MEDIA
STUDIES FOR AQA GCSE

PETER WALL
Chief Examiner

Collins

Published by HarperCollins*Publishers* Limited
77–85 Fulham Palace Rd
Hammersmith
London W6 8JB

www.**Collins**Education.com
Online support for schools and colleges

An imprint of HarperCollins*Publishers*

©HarperCollins*Publishers* 2007

First published 2007

10 9 8 7 6 5 4 3 2 1

Student book: ISBN 978-0-00-723497-4

Teacher's Resource: ISBN 978-0-00-723496-7

Peter Wall asserts the moral right to be identified as the author of this work.

British Library Cataloguing in Publication Data

A catalogue record for this publication is available from the British Library

Design: Paul Manning
Commissioning editor: Charlie Evans
Project management: Gaby Frescura
Production: Simon Moore

Printed and bound by Printing Express, Hong Kong

Contents

Acknowledgements

Realia

Advertising Standards Authority, p.199; Apple Computer, Inc., p.166; www.bbc.co.uk, p.109; ww.blockbuster.co.uk, p.94; The BPI www.bpi.co.uk, p.168; British Board of Film Classification, p.69; www.cosmopolitan.co.uk, p.115; Capital Radio, p.210; Timm Cleasby/Scott Gillies (www.fifty-50.co.uk), p.174; *Daily Express*, p.144; www.diesel.com, p.197; DVD, p.105; *Empire*, p.93; *Glamour*, p.6; www.graziamagazine.co.uk, p.115; Guardian Newspapers Ltd., p.129; Guardian Unlimited, p.136; GQ, pp.6, 115; *Hammersmith and Shepherds Bush Gazette*, p.130; *Heat*, p.151; Heart FM, p.210; *Hotdog*, p.105; *Independent*, p.144; *The Lady*, p.82; *Loaded*, p.82; *London Lite*, p.187; *Loot*, p.189; *Metro*, p.187; Mirror.co.uk, p.114; *The Mirror*, p.145; *Mojo magazine*, p.183; MySpace pp.53, 122; www.nme.com, p.115; *NME*, p.183; Office of Communications, p.216; The Official UK Charts Company, p.179; Pure Digital, pp.110, 207, 209; *Q*, p.183; *Radio Times*, p.111; secondlife.com, p.122; Sky +, p.109; www.smashhits.net, p.117; *The Sun* – www.thesun.co.uk, pp.114, 116; Telegraph.co.uk, p.114; *The Telegraph*, p.145; Times Online, p.116; www.timesmediaadvertising.com, p.190; *Time Out*, p.148; Virgin Radio; Vue cinemas, p.92; XFM, p.210; Marvel Comics, p.160; YouTube, pp.53, 122.

Photos

Advertising Archive, pp.11, 35, 43, 45, 84, 112, 117, 129, 148, 151, 155, 156, 157, 158, 159, 186, 188, 189, 191, 194, 196; Alamy, pp.86, 192; Aquarius, pp.19, 24, 42, 56, 256; BBC Photo Library, pp.30–31, 236, 238, 244, 246; Sky News, pp.2, 118, 205, 220, 221, 222, 224, 225, 227, 228, 231, 232, 233; Corbis, pp.10, 23, 29, 49, 58, 88, 91, 102, 104, 204, 242, 247; Empics, pp.3, 4, 5, 10, 17, 18, 26, 34, 37, 38, 39, 40, 48, 50, 51, 56, 57, 62, 64, 72, 73, 93, 106, 113, 119, 121, 126, 133, 138, 208, 211, 243, 248, 249, 250, 251, 252; Fremantle Media Stills Library, pp.173, 178, 240–241; Getty Images, pp. 65, 67, 68 124; ITV Granada, p.74; Kobal, pp.27, 76, 80, 90, 98; Mary Evans Picture Library, pp.135, 163; Moviestore, pp.96, 101; Photos.com, p.206, 212, 212, 217; Redferns Picture Library, pp.162, 165, 169, 170, 171, 180, 181; Rex Features Picture Library, p.254; Science and Society Picture Library, pp.127, 128, 133, 134.

Illustrations

Katie Mac, pp.20–21; Stephane Gamain, p.46.

Media
Studies

INTRODUCTION

1 Why Media Studies?

There is a powerful force sending its messages to virtually everyone on earth. It is using every form of communication available. It is in your sitting room, your bedroom, maybe even in your bathroom. It is in shops, cinemas, libraries and churches. It travels in cars, on buses, trains, planes and ships. Even if you blast off into space, it is out there waiting for you. No matter how hard you try, you cannot escape it.

The media: monster or angel?

The name of this force is 'the media', and whether you like it or not, it defines your life and the way you think. 'The media' is the name given to channels of communication a society uses to speak for itself. It includes television, cinema, video, radio, newspapers, magazines, books and the internet. In effect the media is a mass of individual contact points between communication tools and human beings.

It is difficult to visualise this, however, and most people speak about the media as if it were a single being with a personality of its own. It has been portrayed more as a monster than as an angel. Television has been criticised for luring schoolchildren away from their homework; videos have been accused of encouraging violence and drug abuse; newspapers and magazines of filling our heads with gossip; and computer games of turning us into goggle-eyed morons. Whatever the problem, it seems the media is in part to blame.

Television has, however, brought information and learning to millions of people, with satellite broadcasting allowing us to experience history as it happens. Videos are widely used as teaching aids in schools and colleges. Radio supplies a lifeline for those cut off from the outside world. Magazines and newspapers provide knowledge as well as entertainment, while computers provide us with an 'information superhighway' that facilitates world-wide communication.

Satellite broadcasting has the potential to reach millions all over the world

Is the media a good thing or a bad thing? As we have seen, the media is not one 'thing', but a large number of interactions between individual receivers and specific media products, or texts; so really, the question is meaningless. Also, judgements about what is 'good, or 'bad' tend to differ between individuals, groups and societies over time. A more helpful approach is to examine media products and ask how they are made, what they contain and what receivers make of them. In doing this, we can begin to understand the part media plays in modern life.

The changing world of the media

It is important to realise that we live at a time when the media itself is undergoing dynamic change. Many of the traditional ways we consume the media are being changed by the new technologies the media uses to deliver its products to us. For example, many homes are now equipped with digital televisions capable of receiving hundreds of television channels and radio stations beamed to us by satellites. Similarly, many homes have powerful personal computers connected to the internet. These computers have the potential to connect us to almost unlimited amounts of information and entertainment delivered direct to our homes.

New technologies are transforming the media

A key aspect of this new technology is that it is interactive. This means that we can influence and even change the nature of the media products we receive. Not only can we select a specific programme to watch, we can even choose the camera angle from which we see it. So, when you watch a football match using digital technology, you have the power to direct the programme from your own armchair. The advent of DVD (Digital Video Disc) offers audiences the choice of selecting a whole range of extras when they buy or rent a film.

Such extras might include the option of replacing the original soundtrack with a commentary by the director or the stars.

You can use your digital television to shop or to get access to your bank account. You can also use it to send and receive emails, just like a personal computer. The technology of digital television and that of the personal computer are now moving even closer together. This is called convergence. It means that a world of information is potentially available to you through your television. With the simple click of a mouse, you are able to obtain just about anything you want. Recently released films can be piped to you on demand. When you consider too the improved quality of television pictures and sound, with large, wide-screen, surround-sound sets, it becomes clear that many of us no longer need to leave the house to go to the cinema, to a football match or even to the shops. Most newspapers and magazines, even, are available to us in online editions, which means we can read them on our computer screens.

It is not only in the home that these technological changes are affecting the way we consume the media. Much of the information and entertainment available at home is becoming accessible through the mobile phone, too. This means that people are also able to enjoy these benefits while on the move.

One of the important concerns of Media Studies is to consider just how these technological changes are likely to influence our lives. It is clear that, as you begin your study of the media, you are doing so at a time when some important and exciting changes are taking place.

This palm-top 'internet tablet' connects to the web via 'wi-fi' or compatible cellular phone

Key concepts

At GCSE you are going to have to get to grips with what we call 'key concepts' for studying the media. These concepts are language, representation, institution and audience. By exploring these concepts you can begin to understand how the media works and the part it plays in our lives.

Look at the magazine covers below. How does considering the key concepts of media help us to understand them?

Each of these magazines offers its own highly selective picture of the world

Language: The covers of magazines use both words and images to communicate with us. These words and images are put together in much the same way as on other magazine covers. Certain conventions have been followed so that we recognise the covers as belonging to magazines. The covers are media messages that have been encoded, and we decode them. This process of communication requires the use of 'media language'. As media students you will be looking at the way in which media products are put together, or constructed. You will learn terminology that will help you analyse them.

Representation: The magazines covers are presenting us with information about the world. *GQ* is telling us, for example, that the hottest woman in the world is Beyoncé. In giving us this information, someone has selected and shaped what we see. The woman on the front cover of *Glamour* is not, in some senses, a real woman, but an image used to represent a woman. This process of presenting information about the world to us is called 'representation'. In looking at this key concept we will be assessing just how accurate media representations are.

Institutions: The magazines have been produced by a media organisation, or 'institution'. This institution has arranged for the magazines to be written, illustrated, put together, printed, advertised and distributed to your local newsagent. This process is called media production. We will be looking at how media institutions work, and at how the way they work can influence the media products they create.

Audience: The people who buy and read the magazines are usually called the 'audience'. We use the word 'audience' to describe consumers of all media products, not just film, television and radio. The audience is important because this is where the media products are targeted. Without an audience, a media product serves little purpose. We will be looking at the nature of media audiences. We will also look at how audiences consume the media and what effect the media has upon the lives of us as audiences.

2 Language

When you hear the word **language** you will probably automatically think of words, either spoken or written. Words are an important part of communication between human beings. But the media does not communicate with words alone. It can also use pictures and sounds to convey meaning. Indeed, some media can work purely in a visual language, through pictures that you can understand in the same way as words.

Aspects of language

Visual language

Photography is an example of a visual medium, or one that relies for its impact on images. Film and television are also visual media, although both use words and sounds as well to communicate information. Print-based media, such as newspapers, magazines and comics employ a combination of printed words and pictures, such as photographs, drawings and graphics, to give you information.

> "Cinema, radio, television, magazines are a school of inattention: people look without seeing, listen in without hearing."
> **Robert Bresson**

Radio, on the other hand, is obviously a medium that relies on the spoken word and other sounds to communicate: it is an aural medium. Pop music, which is a large part of many radio stations' output, conversely carries with it a lot of visual images such as pictures of the bands and CD cover designs.

You sometimes hear people say that we live in a media-saturated society. They mean that everywhere you look, words and images are fighting for your attention and bombarding you with messages. But with so much 'information overload', how much do you really take in?

As small children you learn how to use language. For one thing, it helps other people know what you want. Of course, the vocabulary that you learn will depend on the culture in which you grow up. The words learnt by French children for describing the world are different from those learnt by children in the UK. As you grow up, you also learn to understand visual signs. No one sits down with you and explains how to watch television. Simply by repeatedly watching TV, you learn to make sense of the various short cuts that a visual medium, such as TV, uses to tell you a story more quickly. For example, if a character is shown leaving a room and is seen in the next shot driving a car, the viewer fills in the missing sequence in their imagination and understands that the character has left the house, got into the car and set off.

In the same way that you learn to read words on a page, so you learn to read visual language. The idea of 'reading' is important in Media Studies. When you read a book, you use your imagination to create pictures in your head; you bring something of yourself to the book by working it out in your mind.

Similarly, if you apply the idea of reading to television, it suggests that you are active in bringing something of yourself to it. Just as you use your imagination to fill in the missing parts of a visual narrative to make sense of what has happened, you learn to read other elements of visual language. The way in which you read an image or set of images may well be decided by your upbringing and previous experiences.

Not everyone who watches a set of images on the television will take from them the same meaning. For example, an advertisement that uses an attractive young woman to sell a product may well have a positive impact on many men in the audience. Female viewers with strong opinions about the ways in which women's bodies are exploited by the media are likely to read the advertisement very differently. Similarly, a cookery programme featuring recipes for cooking pork chops would have little appeal to vegetarians or members of certain religious groups. In fact many of them will turn off the programme on the grounds that it is offensive.

In most media, words and pictures work together to create meaning. Very often, words can be used to limit, or anchor, the meaning of a visual image. In newspapers, photographs have captions to tell the reader how to interpret the

In order to make sense of the world, we need to be able to decode visual signs

images. On news bulletins, newsreaders or reporters talk over the images to explain what is happening, which guides the viewers' interpretation of the meaning of the images they see. This process if called 'anchorage'. Just as the anchor of a ship is used to hold it in one place, so the words in a caption or commentary are used to hold or limit the meaning of an image.

This advertisement for mineral water contains a number of meanings, some of which could be offensive to women

Connotation and denotation

Both words and images, it is argued, work on at least two levels:

Denotation The common-sense or everyday meaning of a sign. A red rose, for example, is a garden plant. That is its denotational meaning.

Connotation The additional or associated meaning that an image or word carries with it, over and above its ordinary, everyday meaning. A red rose is a symbol of love. If you give someone a red rose, they are unlikely to think you are simply handing over a garden plant; for someone who lives in Lancashire, it is also the symbol that represents their county.

What is the connotation of this image?

When you 'read' a TV programme, magazine or film, your understanding of these texts relies on your ability to respond to both these layers of meaning at the same time.

Media language

Look at the advertisement on the opposite page. It appeared in various women's magazines including *Easy Living*, which covers such things as 'real life' fashion, homes and food. A magazine of this type addresses women in a number of roles but emphasises their roles in the home as wives and mothers. The advertisement is for a washing tablet, although you may have noticed that nowhere is there any reference to the actual washing of clothes. The first thing you may notice is that it features a man and a child. This is especially significant given the context of the magazine that features the advertisement. Traditionally women are associated with the role of rearing and looking after children. Although such attitudes are changing, the image in the advert – that of a man in the role of child carer – is noticeable because it runs counter to a gender stereotype. In a magazine that is full of images, those that appear in advertisements have to be capable of grabbing our attention and often attempt to do so by presenting us with something that is unexpected or even shocking.

Once the image has got our attention, we can begin to consider what it is about. Think what you notice most about the image when you first look at it. There are a number of possibilities. You may notice that the predominant colour is blue. The man, who is the largest object in the photograph, is dressed in different shades of blue. The sky at the back is a blue grey colour. The text, which is placed at the top of the image against the sky, is also blue. Only the flesh tones, the greenery and the child's white shirt present us with an alternative to the all-pervading blueness of the image. Consider why you think the advertisers have chosen to make blue such a prominent colour.

You might also notice the absence of women and girls in the photograph.

The child appears to be a young boy sitting on his father's chest. His mother is absent from the image, although her presence may be quite strongly implied. Notice too how the child and the man are bound up in each other, unaware of the camera which is taking their photograph. The man's body language is relaxed. His pose is casual. His gaze is directed towards his son. He is smiling and looking at the child with love and affection. The pose is one in which the man seems protective towards the child and proud of him. This is further emphasised by the contrast in the size of the two figures. The man is

Is gentle something you touch or something that touches you?

Ariel Sensitive.
The name says it all. It's gentle next to skin, even the British Allergy Foundation has endorsed it.
www.arielsensitive.co.uk

Is gentle something you touch or something that touches you?
Ariel Sensitive.
The name says it all. It's gentle next to skin, even the British Allergy Foundation has endorsed it.
ARIEL

A spontaneous snapshot from a family album?

large, filling much of the frame; the child in contrast is small, perched on top of his father. Note too that the young boy is preoccupied, clutching with both hands at his father's shirt. You will see that the man is dressed casually. His shirt has short sleeves and is worn outside of his denim jeans. We can assume he is a man relaxing in the company of his young son.

The photograph looks very much like a spontaneous snapshot from a family album. This is how we are meant to see it – as a casual celebration of a warm and caring man who is delighting in his young son and enjoying spending time with him. The two are in an outdoor setting in the countryside or a park. You might like to think about the connotations of the setting. We associate being outdoors with a healthy lifestyle and the countryside or a park with the idea of relaxing away from the hustle and bustle of our daily lives.

A photograph like this presents to us a single moment in an ongoing narrative. On a connotational level we may feel the need to work out for ourselves the 'before' and 'after' of this narrative. How did the man and the boy come to be lying on the grass together? Where will they go when they have finished? You could make up your own narrative to fill in these details, but for most people it would inevitably involve a home and a wife/mother.

Indeed it is these elements which are missing from the image that potentially speak to us most powerfully. The man and boy are happy together. Their clothes are clean and they are well presented. They both appear 'looked after' and 'cared for'. The connotation is that the wife and mother, despite being absent from the image, is the force that makes them happy and content with life. It is this absent woman's laundry skills and her good sense in choosing an appropriate cleaning product that have given these males their sense of well-being and contentment. They may occupy centre stage, but it is her work behind the scenes that enables them to do so with such confidence.

Printed words in an advertisement of this sort have the function of anchoring the meaning that the reader can take from it. The words limit the ways in which we can interpret the image. However, in this example the words present us with an enigma or riddle. 'Is gentle something you touch or something that touches you?' Notice the rather odd nature of the typeface here. This seems to be a typeface especially created for this advertisement and appears to represent little bits of cotton or stitching. You will notice how longer pieces trail from the 'o' in 'something' and the question mark, rather like the strings on a balloon flying through the sky. What these words mean and how they link to the image is far from clear. We are being deliberately presented with this enigma as a problem to solve. We are being asked to answer a question to which there is no obvious answer. This makes the advertisement more open to interpretation and invites the reader to offer their own individual way of reading it. Part of the ambivalence or openness of the advertisement comes from the fact that the word 'touch' can be read in at least two different ways. Firstly the word means simply to make physical contact with someone else. The child is touching the man's shirt. Secondly touch also implies a sense of being emotionally affected by something. We are touched by the close bond that the father and son clearly have. You might like to think how the advertising copywriter intends us to interpret the words.

Again looking at the way in which printed words are used, the actual information about the product is relatively insignificant in relation to the image that dominates the page. The brand name Ariel Sensitive is given to us at the foot of the page in bold type. Then a brief explanation is offered that the name of the product tells us all we need to know. This is followed by an ungrammatical sentence which tells us that the product is gentle next to skin and has been endorsed by the British Allergy Foundation. Next to this we see the foundation's seal of approval, together with another seeming endorsement that the product has been 'dermatologically tested'. Beneath is a URL, which may offer us more information, and at the right of the page a picture of the product itself. You will again notice this preponderance of blue in the writing and the image of the product. You should also see that the typeface used, in contrast to the one in the image, is very clear, clean and modern.

What does this all add up to? Little that you see in an advertisement like this has been included by chance. Advertising costs large sums of money and advertisers must ensure that they get things right. Photographs are carefully staged and shot. Words are carefully chosen by copywriters to have the right impact. The relationship between words and images is carefully thought through. In general it is reasonable to assume that a specific advertiser has thought very carefully about the impact they want to have on the reader. Advertising most especially of all media forms plays upon our hidden desires. Often we are not even conscious of these when we look at an advertisement, as they work on a subconscious level.

In this example there are strong connotations at play. The image powerfully communicates to us the idea of contentment and happiness. Happiness here is to be found in the form of the love of a father for his son. The question we must ask concerns the context and the audience for the advertisement. It is presented to us in a magazine aimed at women, along with other advertisements and editorial content aimed in some part in supporting women as wives and mothers. It is as though the advertisement is offering for our view some ideal that a woman can achieve by ensuring that the clothes she washes are clean. That ideal is a happy family; a father and son who can play contentedly together, lying together on the grass, happy in the knowledge that there is a wife, mother and washing powder at home that will always ensure that they can go out into the world looking their best.

Texts

The term 'media text' refers to any product of the media – anything from a magazine article to a quiz show, for example. The word 'text' has important connotations when used in an educational context. Because English literature has been such an important part of the curriculum for so many years, the word 'text' is often associated with literary texts. Texts are the books you may study as part of your English course. Often these will be classics of English literature, representing high levels of achievement by great writers. *Hamlet, Pride and Prejudice, Wuthering Heights* and *Great Expectations* are texts in this sense. Because of this connotation of the word 'text', calling a quiz show a text may seem a little

To appreciate a highly stylised art form such as classical ballet, you need to be familiar with its codes and conventions

strange. Some people may argue that a quiz show is trivial compared to the great classics of English literature. But this concept of texts is important. Just as the classics of English literature are studied, so you study and analyse a soap opera in order to learn about the society in which you live. If that idea seems a little silly, then remember that in his lifetime Shakespeare's plays would have been performed in pubs, with all social classes crowding in to watch them. It is now a common idea that Shakespeare is of interest only to an elite, but that was certainly not true when the plays were first written. This is not to suggest that *Coronation Street* or *Neighbours* will one day have the importance of *Othello* or *Silas Marner*. The argument is that by studying these texts, we can learn a lot about the lives and culture of the people who consume them.

This argument can be taken one step further: the more texts you study, the better you become at reading them. For example, if you were to go to the ballet for first time, you might find it hard to understand what it was all about. People who go to the ballet regularly would have learned the codes and conventions that ballet uses and, in most cases, would easily follow what was going on. The same is true of people who go to the cinema regularly: they are likely to be very good at reading films. They may spot jokes, for instance, in the references that one film makes to another, which those who go to the cinema less often would probably miss.

As you can see, the words 'read' and 'text' themselves have important connotations. In the chapter on audience (see pages 64–87), the way the media affects people is discussed. The word 'read' implies a reader who is actively involved in the text. Just as with a book, readers of other media texts are contributing to the meaning that the text makes, by means of their involvement with it. This is obviously a long way from the common picture of the passive TV viewer, who mindlessly consumes whatever images are displaying on the screen.

Codes

To most people the word 'code' stands for a secret method of communicating, which must be cracked or decoded so that the hidden message can be understood. Numbers or symbols, for instance, may be used instead of letters of the alphabet; until you work out how to decipher the code, the message will have no meaning. Language itself is a code: the words in a particular language have meanings because everyone who speaks that language uses them in roughly the same way to mean roughly the same thing.

Each medium has its own code. Once you have learned the code, you can understand the meaning. For example, the music that is played at the beginning of a news bulletin is part of a code. It is serious music that sounds important and calls the viewer to the TV set, in just the same way as a town crier used to ring a bell and shout 'Oyez' to summon an audience to hear an important announcement. There are other codes at work in a news bulletin. Well-spoken, well-dressed people sit behind a desk in a studio and tell viewers about the world. They introduce other people, tell the viewers what is happening and show them pictures of events that have taken place. Sometimes the

A TV weather map requires viewers to understand and decode a set of visual symbols

viewer can hear only the presenter's or reporter's voice, while at other times he or she talks directly to the viewer. All these are codes that TV uses to communicate with viewers. They come to form a convention, or an accepted way of doing things that people are used to and have learned to recognise. For example, there is a convention that the news appears at fixed times every day and that certain people will present it in a specific way. Because of these conventions, if you switch on your TV set halfway through the news, you don't think you're watching a quiz show. We will look further at these concepts later in this chapter under the heading of 'Genre' (see pages 30–33).

The theme music, opening credits and set design of the TV quiz show Who Wants To Be A Millionnaire *all form part of an instantly recognisable code*

IMAGE ANALYSIS
Making an image

The study of how images are put together, and how the audience takes meaning from them, is called image analysis. The factors that affect 'still' photographs also apply to moving images on film or television. Imagine that a friend has asked you to take their photograph. Before you take the photograph, there are a number of decisions you will make – consciously or otherwise.

The long shot

SHOTS

One important decision is how large you want the subject to be relative to the frame. The size of an image within the frame has various technical names according to how close the camera is to the subject

The medium shot

The close-up shot

The long shot (LS) shows the subject in their environment or context. The subject only takes up a small amount of the frame. In film and TV this is sometimes called an establishing shot, because it establishes where a character is. An establishing shot is often used at the beginning of a sequence to give the audience an idea of the setting or context the character is in.

The medium shot (MS) usually shows the top half of someone's body. A roughly equal amount of the frame is given to the subject and the setting. This shot is commonly used when TV reporters are speaking to the camera – outside 10 Downing Street, for example – so that both the reporter and the setting are noticeable.

The close-up shot (CU) shows head and shoulders. The subject fills most of the screen and you can see a great deal of detail in his or her face. This is a good shot for showing emotion and creating a strong feeling of intimacy with the subject.

The big close-up (BCU) shows the face of the subject filling the whole of the frame. This is a powerful shot for showing strong feelings, such as someone in tears.

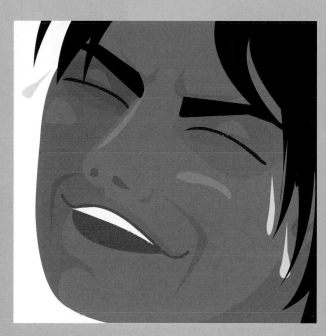

The big close-up shot

The point-of-view shot

Point-of-view shot – see the section on point of view (pages 25–26).

ANGLE

Another decision you will make before you take your photograph is the angle at which you will hold the camera.

You may have noticed that images are usually shot at eye-level, so that the camera and the subject are on the same level. This creates a feeling that the viewer is equal with the subject.

A **high-angle shot** allows the viewer to look down on the subject, which gives a sense of superiority.

A **low-angle shot** has the opposite effect. The viewer is invited to look up at the subject, which may make the viewer feel uncomfortable or dominated.

OTHER FACTORS

Several other factors will also influence each shot:

Setting Where will the photographs be taken – in a back garden, in the street or in a studio? The setting of the photograph will influence how it is interpreted. In film-making, it is very important to decide on the setting, that is, what will take place in front of the camera and how it will be shot. These considerations are known as the 'mise-en-scene'.

Framing Once you have chosen the setting, the next job is to frame the shot. This means that you have to decide how your subject will be positioned with the photograph. You do this by looking through the viewfinder until you get the best image for your purpose.

Continued on page 22

IMAGE ANALYSIS

Making an image contd

Focus Is everything sharply in focus, or are some parts of the image blurred? If so, is the blurring deliberate?

Colour Is the photograph in colour or black and white? Are there reasons for this choice? If the photo is in colour, what sort of colours are most obvious: bright colours or duller ones? Do the colours blend well together?

Lighting How is the image lit? Is natural lighting used, or artificial light such as from a flashgun? Backlighting, where the chief source of light is from behind the central figure, can have a strong impact, as can sidelighting, where one side of a person's face is lit and the other side is in shadow.

Pose and body languagee How are the figures displayed within the frame? Are they posed or do they look natural? Have they been caught in action, or lined up for the camera?

Composition How have the different elements that make up the photograph been put together? When you look at any photo, think about where you look first. What does your eye see first in the picture and where is it led? Is it drawn to the most important detail in the photograph? If there is a group of people, who seems to be the most important one – the one that catches your eye?

THE MOVING IMAGE

The movie camera is often regarded as an all-seeing eye, which observes without being observed. It is able to follow the action wherever it takes place. It can stalk people, following them without their knowledge, and it can peep through windows. The fact that the camera as well as the subject can move allows the creation of images that are more complex and dynamic than still photographs. Two shots that enable it to do this are:

- **The pan**, in which the camera moves horizontally, either following a piece of action or shifting across from one image to another, as though making a survey of the scene.

- **The zoom,** where the camera zooms in from a long shot to a big close-up, moving in to inspect what is going on.

These effects show the power of the camera to control the action within the frame, either by holding an image as it moves, or by seeking out subjects that are part of the action.

Editing

If you are making a film or a video, another series of decisions has to be made once the images have been recorded. This is called editing, which is the process of putting the images together in a logical sequence. An editor links the scenes by using a range of devices intended to shift the viewer's attention from one scene to another.

The cut is where one scene ends and another begins immediately. This is probably the most frequently used of all the edits. An audience is likely to read this device to mean that all the action is taking place in a normal time sequence, or that one scene follows on logically and chronologically from another.

The fade is where the picture slowly disappears until the screen is blank (usually black). After a fade, a new scene may be started by fading up, which is when an image slowly appears from a blank screen. The audience might read this device to mean that a period of time has passed in between the two scenes. A shot that finishes in the evening, for

"The editing makes the movie."
Garry Marshall

example, will often be followed by one that fades up the next morning.

The dissolve is where one scene fades out as a new scene fades in. It is possible to freeze these images on a video recorder and see both scenes mixed into a single frame in the middle of a dissolve. This device is another method of showing that time has passed, or that people have moved on – in a journey, say. The dissolve is also commonly used when landscape images, such as a misty morning, are set to music to give gentle, romantic views of the countryside, for example.

The wipe is where a new scene wipes over an existing scene from one side of the screen to the other. This kind of edit sharply shifts the viewer's attention from one scene to another. It is especially effective at suggesting that parallel action is taking place elsewhere. Technology has enabled film and TV programme makers to produce a whole range of more elaborate methods of switching scenes, many of which are based on the wipe – for example, a scene folding up and disappearing into the ear of a character in the next scene.

Another job that an editor performs is the linking together of sounds and images. Moving images are usually accompanied by sounds. These may be in the form of music to create atmosphere; they may be sounds

related to what we see on the screen, such as people speaking to each other, which is known as dialogue; or they may be sound effects, such as explosions. Alternatively, the soundtrack may take the form of an off-screen commentary, known as a voice-over.

This section has concentrated on how photographs and moving images have codes and conventions, which the viewer learns to read in order to make sense of them. Obviously this is also true of other media forms. The case study on newspapers (see pages 126–146) looks at how page layout works as a code that suggests to the reader how to read the page.

Jack Nicholson
in the suspense
classic The Shining

Narratives

Words and pictures are often combined in media texts in order to create narratives. Narratives are basically stories. From our earliest years, we enjoy narratives, whether in the form of a story told at bedtime to send us off to sleep, or a story told to our class at the end of a hard day at primary school. These stories are sometimes offered as a reward for good behaviour or are withheld as a punishment for being naughty. As we grow up, the link between stories and behaviour is therefore mixed in our minds. Narratives themselves are often about rewards or punishments for the ways that people behave.

Narratives are important to people. One reason is that they help to make sense of the world. Religious books, for example, are full of stories that attempt to explain the disasters that afflict the human race. The actual number of possible narratives is, however, limited. New stories are uncommon: most narratives are variations on a limited number of timeless themes. The characters and settings may vary, but the structure remains the same.

Suspense

If stories occur so frequently, why don't people get bored with them? One reason is that narratives take different forms according to their settings and the characters used to tell the story. They do not simply retell a story that has been told many times before: their effects are more complex. An important element in any narrative is suspense, which is the feeling of excitement or anxiety that you have as you wait for something to happen. Suspense is an example of what is called 'narrative code'. This is a way of describing the conventions or elements that an audience expects to be included in a story. Suspense works by means of a device called an enigma, which is a puzzle or a riddle. A good narrative teases the audience by giving clues about what will happen next, or making the audience try to work out the answer to the puzzle. Murder mysteries and detective stories are popular across a range of media (such as films, TV, comics and magazines) because they work by teasing their audience. Cliff-hangers, likewise, are key elements of soaps. Originally the term 'cliff-hanger' described a situation when, at the end of an episode, a character was left dangling – either literally or metaphorically – over the edge of a cliff. Cliff-hangers keep the audience guessing what will happen in the next episode.

Enigmas also play an important role in non-fiction texts. For example, the news begins with headlines, which tease the viewer with information to get them to stay tuned to find out more. Newspaper headlines whet the reader's appetite for the story: they contain teasing clues about the narrative to follow.

Point of view

Another aspect of narrative structure is the point of view from which the audience sees the story. Many films and television programmes are about the eternal battle between good and evil. The audience is usually encouraged to identify with the good characters, and wants them to win. In a police series, for example, the viewer is invited to watch the action from the point of view of the police officer, who is trying to solve a crime and put a criminal behind bars for the protection of society.

Narratives are constructed to ensure that most of the audience will respond in a certain way. One way of placing the viewer alongside the hero or good character is to let the audience see what the hero sees. The viewer shares information with the hero. The hero may even speak directly to them through a voice-over, which allows the audience to share his or her thoughts and feelings.

As you watch a film or TV programme, note how often the camera shows you what the hero sees. The camera becomes the hero's eyes and gives the audience the same privileged view as that of the hero. This shot is called the 'point-of-view' shot and is a very important way of 'positioning' the audience alongside a specific character. A device called a Steadicam has been developed, which allows a camera operator to film while walking or even running and yet keep the shot steady. Steadicams and lightweight video equipment have increased the opportunities for using 'point-of-view' shots. A programme such as *The Bill* places the audience right alongside the police as they raid houses or chase suspects.

What is the difference in point of view in these two images?

Needless to say, it is not only fictional programmes that tell the story from the viewpoint of one character. When conflict is taking place between the police and the community, for example, the news often shows pictures shot behind a line of police officers.

Conflict

The idea of conflict is important in narratives. Many stories are framed as a fight between two people or two groups. In fiction this is often depicted as a conflict between good and evil. In Westerns, peace-loving communities are frequently threatened by outlaws. The conflict is often resolved by a gunman. Gangster films present a conflict between society and those who flout its laws and values. Narratives based on conflict are found in many unlikely places. Many wildlife programmes are structured as narratives. The plot may rely on conflict between animals that hunt and those that are hunted. The side that the audience supports is often determined by the viewpoint of the group of animals that is 'starring' in the show. In this way, even natural born killers can be presented in a sympathetic light.

The audience is often invited to take sides in narrative conflict, often that of good against evil

The audience is invited to take sides in the conflict, usually supporting the forces of 'good' and against those of 'evil'. In the media's coverage of the news, this has important effects, especially in the presentation of stories about politics or international relations. It is often said that the news on television and radio should be unbiased. This means that it should avoid taking sides in a dispute and should simply present the different viewpoints, allowing the audience to form its own opinion. In reality, however, the coverage of such major events as football games on television or in the press may encourage the

audience to support one side against the other. In the same way, in responding to the manner in which the news is presented, most people will inevitably take up a position in favour of one viewpoint.

When the UK is at war or in conflict with other countries, the narrative is often told from the viewpoint that the UK is right and its opponents are wrong. Battles are seen from behind British lines, looking towards the enemy (see Chapter 5, pages 64–87). Some people argue that the same is true of industrial disputes: strikers may form part of a narrative in which they are pictured as disruptive forces trying to stop peace-loving people getting on with their lives.

> "The media's the most powerful entity on earth. They have the power to make the innocent guilty and to make the guilty innocent, and that's power. Because they control the minds of the masses." **Malcolm X**

Motivation

Characters and their motivation are extremely important in narratives. As we have already seen, the audience is often invited to see the action through the eyes of one particular character. This character is defined as the hero.

All the main characters will have a motivation, a reason for doing something that drives them to achieve their aim. This motivation may take the form of a goal they set out to achieve. It may be to catch a criminal, to win the heart of a person they have fallen for, or maybe just to have a good time. Some characters go in search of themselves, or on a similar quest. These goals may bring them into conflict with other characters, whose goals are in opposition to theirs – a criminal who doesn't want to get caught, for example, or a man or a woman who doesn't want to be won, or a person who doesn't want the hero to have a good time. The viewer's interest in this narrative is, of course, to discover whether or not the hero manages to achieve his or her goal.

Ideology

We experience narrative from childhood onwards. Narrative also plays a key role in forming our social behaviour and attitudes in later life. There is much debate about the ideas of good and evil, and especially about the question of whose job it is to teach young children about right and wrong. The concepts of good and evil, right and wrong, are key elements of television programmes,

> "Thomas Jefferson once said: 'Of course the people don't want war. But the people can be brought to the bidding of their leader. All you have to do is tell them they're being attacked and denounce the pacifists for somehow a lack of patriotism and exposing the country to danger. It works the same in any country.' I think that was Jefferson. Oh wait. That was Hermann Goering. Shoot." **Jon Stewart**

newspapers and even pop music. It is argued that people learn their value systems from these media; they present an ideology, a system of belief by which people organise their lives.

An important part of growing up is learning to see narrative as both a reward and a way of teaching good behaviour. For example, you may learn to believe that if you work hard and don't argue with people in authority, then you will be rewarded; bad behaviour will be punished. The problem lies in who decides what is good and bad. Many people in authority have a strong interest in encouraging the belief that obedience and respect for people in superior positions is good behaviour. Can you trust the people who control the media to work in your best interests?

In Nazi Germany in the 1930s, the media was used as a powerful instrument of propaganda. Among other devices, it used narratives to persuade ordinary people that those from different ethnic backgrounds were the cause of evil in the world. Sadly, many people were taken in by these lies. In other words, narrative is a powerful means of getting over ideas that can have an impact on people's behaviour. One reason for examining narrative in Media Studies is to make you more aware of its effects and so perhaps less easily influenced by it.

L to R: Nazi leaders Joseph Goebbels, Hermann Goering and Rudolf Hess. As Propaganda Minister, Goebbels used the media as a powerful instrument to promote Nazi ideology

Genre

In order to hold the narrative of a film or television programme together, a scriptwriter will often seek a device that allows the characters to explore their ambitions. The road movie is an ideal form for a journey of self-exploration, an adventure in which the characters can find their true identity.

Disaster films bring people together, for instance on a ship or in a burning building, so that conflicts and ambitions can be played out against a dramatic backdrop. Soaps represent a series of neighbourhood locations in which the characters meet, and the narrative can develop through the reactions of the characters to each other. The pub is a popular meeting place in soaps – far more than in real life!

In other words, narrative can take different forms according to the type of film, TV series or news report in which it appears. Each form has its own conventions, or common practices, and different types of programme can be identified by looking at the conventions used. The types or categories into which the different texts can be fitted are known as genres. The idea of genres allows you to group texts together so that you can study them and develop ideas about how they work. For example, the Western has already been mentioned as a particular genre of film. A list can be drawn up of the distinctive features of the Western: the use of guns and horses, for example, distinguishes this genre from that of, say, the musical; also, the setting of most Westerns can be identified as the Wild West; conflict with the American Indian is another feature of the genre; and many films show the American Indians as savages who threaten the white man's attempt to bring civilisation to the West.

These examples of genre show that it is a useful device for examining media texts and identifying the characteristics that are common to groups of them. Of course, it is a useful concept not only to students of media texts, but also to institutions and

Soaps such as Eastenders are a recognisable genre which has proved enduringly popular

consumers of the texts – the audience. It allows the producer to identify a formula that the audience will find attractive and want to consume. If a film or TV programme has been successful, then there is a reasonable chance that one made to a similar formula will also be successful. Of course this isn't always true: the cinema and TV are littered with unsuccessful sequels and rip-offs of blockbusters.

For the audience, the advantage of identifying a text as belonging to a certain genre is that it highlights it as something they are likely to find enjoyable. For example, films are often advertised as being similar to or even better than another film of the same type. This draws the attention of the audience to similarities and gives them certain expectations about the style and content of the text. It also provides a short cut for audiences, because they have already learnt the conventions by which the genre works. The character types may be familiar and predictable, as may many of the storylines. Viewing within a recognised genre, therefore, will not be such hard work as learning the rules of a new one. This is probably one reason why common forms of TV genre, such as soaps and sitcoms, prove so lastingly popular.

Clearly genre is a concept that can be used more widely than simply putting media texts in groups or categories. It is important that genre is not fixed. The characteristics of a genre are likely to change over a period of time. If you compare an episode of an early police series such as *Dixon of Dock Green*, first broadcast in 1955, with a contemporary series such as *Waking the Dead* or *CSI*, the differences may well be greater than the similarities.

One other important quality of genre is that new genres evolve and old genres become less popular and even disappear. The variety show typified by *Sunday Night at the London Palladium*, popular throughout the 1960s, has largely disappeared from prime-time television viewing (although there has been a minor revival of the genre in *Ant and Dec's Saturday Night Takeaway*). New genres are often created by the fusing together of existing genres. These are called hybrids, after the botanical term used to describe the cross-breeding of plants. A typical hybrid is the docu-soap. This relatively new genre is based on elements of the documentary, such as the realistic recording of the events in people's lives. It also contains qualities we expect to find in a soap opera. These include the focus on individual characters across several episodes, ongoing narratives, and a location that has a sense of community in which people live or work together.

As a means of analysing media texts, the idea of genre has its limitations. One problem is that you can easily go round in a circle: soaps belong to the soap genre because they have the qualities that soaps have. This tells you neither why soaps are so popular, nor what you can expect to learn from studying them. Another problem with the concept of genre is that it does not acknowledge the individual's contribution to a text. This is especially a problem with films, where a director may have a distinctive style of making films in the same way that a novelist has a distinctive style of writing books. For example, Alfred Hitchcock made many thrillers. Other well-known film directors, such as Woody Allen, Jane Campion, Francis Ford Coppola, Spike Lee, David Lynch and Quentin Tarantino all bring their own personal signatures to the genres in which they have worked.

However, media texts are more generally the products of people working together in teams for an organisation – for instance, a newspaper or radio

station – rather than the creation of an individual. Even a book such as this one relies on a team of editors, designers, photographers and production staff to work on the words that the writers have produced before it is ready to be sold. The organisations that these people work for are called media institutions.

REVIEW

In this chapter you have learned about the importance of visual language in considering media products, and about the idea of connotation. You should know that media products communicate with us using codes which we have to learn in order to make meanings from them. You will understand that narrative, which determines how a media product is organised, is important in determining how we respond to a product. Finally we looked at the concept of genre and how it is used to link together products that share similar characteristics.

3 Representation

Representation is the act of communicating by using symbols – for example, using a stick-man to stand for a person. Usually representation takes the form of words, images or symbols. If I give you an apple, I have given you an apple; if I give you a picture of an apple, I have given you a representation of an apple. The difference between reality and representation of reality is not difficult to understand. What is not so obvious is that representation is an act or process in which reality is transformed.

Representation and mediation

The picture I give you might be a photograph, a painting or even a drawing of an apple. The drawing might be a detailed still-life, or it could be a simple outline. Or I might convey the idea of the fruit by using the word 'apple'. The message you get in each case will be 'apple'. What you think about the apple, however, depends to a large degree on how I represent it. If I want to sell you an apple, I might give you a photograph of the best apple I can find and use computer techniques to make it look even better. If I were an artist and wished to suggest the idea of sickness, I might paint a rotting apple as an image to represent a corrupt organisation by describing it as 'rotten to the core'. In each case, the idea of 'apple' will have been worked on to help it convey a meaning. The process of working on an idea or image to convey a specific meaning is called mediation, and it is central to our understanding of media messages.

> "It is not a matter of what is true that counts, but a matter of what is perceived to be true." **Henry Kissinger**

Selecting and structuring representations

Apples have been represented very differently in these two fruit advertisements from different eras

Imagine that, on your way home one day, you see a car crash. A car and a van have collided. There is steam coming from the engines. The van driver is sitting at the side of the road and has blood pouring from his head. Another person is being helped into an ambulance. Traffic in both directions has been stopped by the police. A fire engine arrives and you assume there must be a person trapped in the wreckage. You hear someone say that the car driver pulled out in front of the van without looking. But someone else says that the car had priority. Everywhere you look there is something going on.

When you get home you tell your family what you saw. But do you? If you told them everything you saw, it would take a long time and they would probably get bored. So what you do is select the most interesting facts to tell them. If you told them these facts in the order you experienced them, you would also run the risk of losing your audience. You are more likely to say, 'As I was walking up the road I noticed the police had stopped the traffic, and as I got closer I saw an ambulance and what looked like steam rising into the air. Eventually I saw a van and a car had crashed.' In other words, you reorganise and edit the information so that it has more impact. You may also take a stand on the cause of the accident: 'I thought it was the car driver's fault.' What you have done is to give your own representation of the events you witnessed.

The process you have carried out can be illustrated by the diagram below.

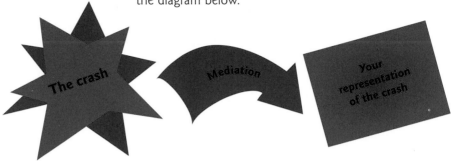

The crash → Mediation → Your representation of the crash

Now imagine you were a journalist reporting the same crash. The process you would go through to produce your report would be very similar. You would select what you saw as the most relevant or interesting aspects of the event, and arrange them into a story that would hopefully attract the attention of your audience.

Versions of reality

It is important to understand that every report of an event, be it a conversation or a media report, is a representation (or RE-presentation) of the event, not a 'presentation' of reality. If we think in terms of the media, reading a newspaper story is equivalent to reading a letter about an event. Listening to a radio report is like receiving a phone call about the event. In both cases, it is easy to see how what you learn about the event is largely controlled by the person writing the letter or making the call – it is their representation of the happening.

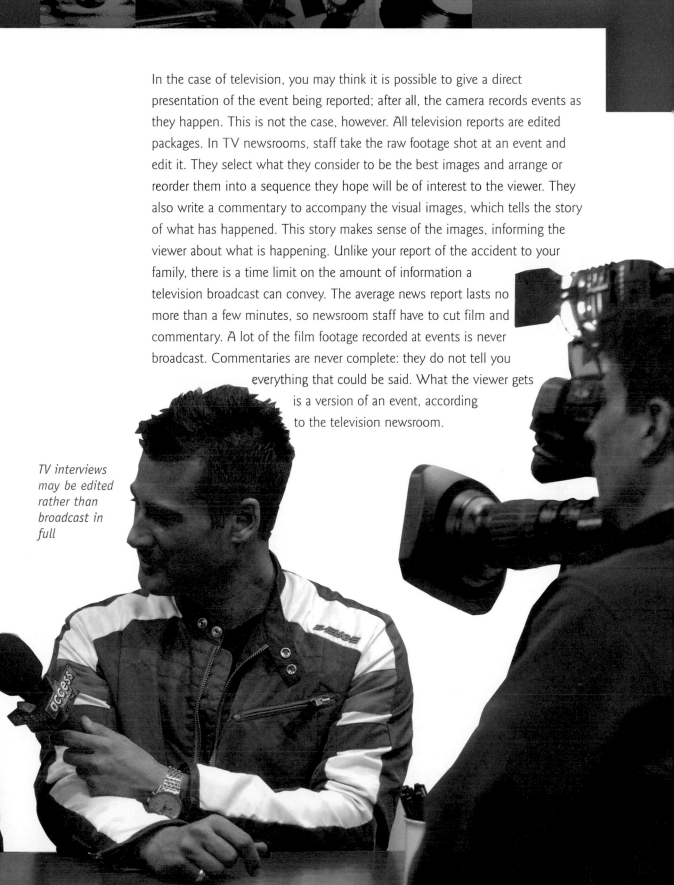

In the case of television, you may think it is possible to give a direct presentation of the event being reported; after all, the camera records events as they happen. This is not the case, however. All television reports are edited packages. In TV newsrooms, staff take the raw footage shot at an event and edit it. They select what they consider to be the best images and arrange or reorder them into a sequence they hope will be of interest to the viewer. They also write a commentary to accompany the visual images, which tells the story of what has happened. This story makes sense of the images, informing the viewer about what is happening. Unlike your report of the accident to your family, there is a time limit on the amount of information a television broadcast can convey. The average news report lasts no more than a few minutes, so newsroom staff have to cut film and commentary. A lot of the film footage recorded at events is never broadcast. Commentaries are never complete: they do not tell you everything that could be said. What the viewer gets is a version of an event, according to the television newsroom.

TV interviews may be edited rather than broadcast in full

TV coverage of sporting events is highly selective

Even in the broadcast of live events, such as football matches, the coverage is 'edited'. You are shown only what is in the camera shot, which is directed by the camera operator. The camera operator decides to film one part of the action rather than another and controls what the viewer will see. Most sporting events, however, are presented in the form of highlights, and, as many football fans who attend games will know, it is very easy to make one side look superior to another by careful selection of film footage. When you consider the selection and reordering that goes into all forms of representation, it becomes obvious that representations are 'versions' of events, not events in themselves.

The same goes for so called reality television. The name given to this genre seems to promise us that what we are seeing is in some way real, and the fact that programmes like *Big Brother* are available to us online 24 hours a day suggests that nothing is selected or edited out. The cameras show us what is there. However, you would not have to spend very much time watching a reality television show to realise that what we see on our screens is just as manipulated as other programmes that do not claim to be 'reality'. You can read more about this in Chapter 13.

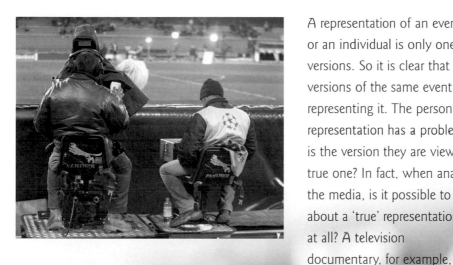

A representation of an event, an issue, a group or an individual is only one of many possible versions. So it is clear that there must be other versions of the same event and other ways of representing it. The person viewing the representation has a problem, therefore: is the version they are viewing the true one? In fact, when analysing the media, is it possible to talk about a 'true' representation at all? A television documentary, for example, appears to offer us a representation of the world as it exists. We call this 'realism'. But we also look upon soap operas as examples of realism, although they are works of fiction performed by actors. To find out if it is possible to talk about a 'true' representation, the factors that influence the production or representations must be studied.

REC
TC 00:02:06:24   Z97

                         MF95
SQU
                         F6.8

                58min

Whose truth?

Imagine your family photograph album. It is full of pictures of you at different stages of your life. Each picture is a representation of you and gives anyone looking at it information on which to base ideas about the type of person you are. Suppose you had to choose one photograph from the album to represent the image of you that you would like a stranger to have. It is a fair bet that you would choose one that shows you as a really cool character, wearing your most fashionable clothes. One thing is certain: the photograph you would pick of yourself would be different from the one your parents would choose to show to a stranger. They would undoubtedly select one of you looking smart and sensible to create what they would see as a 'good impression'. You would probably reject their choice as embarrassing and not a 'true' representation of yourself. Who would be right?

Katie Price, alias media celebrity Jordan

In analysing the media, the issue is not so much who is right, but rather what makes people choose to represent events, issues, groups and individuals in certain ways. Think about you and your family: it is clear that you both have an interest in how you are portrayed to a stranger. Your family would doubtless wish strangers to see a pleasant, well-brought-up person, who is a credit to them. You, on the other hand, would probably want strangers to see you as a streetwise individual with obvious character.

You might like to think about the way in which people like to create images or representations of themselves in order to court popularity with other people. This is especially true of celebrities and the way in which they manipulate their own images in order to attract the attention of the public. This, in turn, has implications for the audiences themselves, many of whom see celebrities as people for whom they have affection or even consider to be role models. The issue of identity and the media is a complex one. Consider, for example, a celebrity like Jordan, who portrays herself as two different people. She has often used her real name, Katie Price, to distinguish herself from the media creation, Jordan, and ran under that name as a parliamentary candidate in the 2001 general election.

What if you were a politician and your parents were the owners of a national newspaper that supported the opposition party? The interests that would influence the choice of representation in this case are obvious. It is in your favour to portray yourself as a person who is in tune with the views of most voters. Your parents, however, as supporters of your opponents, would wish to portray you as someone who is out of step with most people; they might even try to depict you as a danger to the country, to persuade readers of their newspaper not to vote for you.

This is an example of bias. Bias usually results from a person having some kind of relationship with the person or thing they are biased in favour of. For example, if you were selling a car, a potential buyer would probably not believe everything you said about it because you stand to make money by striking a deal; they would say your representation of the car was biased.

Virtually every area of the media has been criticised for the way it represents people and issues. It has been pointed out, for example, that heroes in action and adventure films have traditionally been male; only recently have films with women as the central characters begun to appear. This fact has been seen as a representation of the old-fashioned view that women are not as intelligent,

In the Bond movies, actress Judi Dench took over the traditionally male role of M, head of the British Secret Intelligence Service, in 1995

brave and esourceful as men, and should concern themselves with children and housework. What is called sexism (or prejudice against people because of their sex) has also been pinpointed in the way women are represented in the national press and in advertising. A woman's dress sense and appearance tend to be given attention by the press regardless of why the woman is in the news. Some people say that this means that women are not taken as seriously by the press as men are, and that as a result their views are given less weight.

You should also realise that such representations are not necessarily fixed for all time. Some would argue that women are represented much more positively in the media than they were twenty years ago. Certainly, if you look back at advertising on television, radio and print, there has been a general shift in the way in which women are both represented and addressed. To some extent, this is down to such changes as equal opportunities legislation, which makes it illegal to discriminate on the grounds of gender, but it also reflects economic, social and political change as advertisers see women as having a much more significant role in society generally.

Women have traditionally been used in advertising to sell products. This is especially the case when the product is aimed at men. Car adverts in magazines and on television have traditionally shown a man driving and have included images of an attractive young woman. The message is that if you are male, driving the car will make you attractive to females. Adverts for household goods, on the other hand, such as cleaning materials and food, have traditionally been aimed at women. This can be seen as a reflection of the old-fashioned view that a woman's place is in the home. It has generally been the case that in advertising women have been shown as passive, while men have been portrayed as active and adventurous.

"There are only three ages for women in Hollywood – Babe, District Attorney, and Driving Miss Daisy." **Goldie Hawn**

In the past, car adverts were aimed almost exclusively at men

Representations change with the times, however, and the move towards gender equality has had an effect on how men and women are represented in adverts. More women are now shown driving cars, while men are sometimes shown working in the kitchen and taking care of children.

Content analysis

One method of examining how people are represented in the media is called 'content analysis'. This method measures the number of times a particular representation occurs and draws conclusions about it. For example, a content analyst might count the number of women police officers portrayed in crime dramas; if they were to discover that very few women are represented as police officers, they would ask why this is. Is it because the media is sexist and men are seen as more interesting than women? Or does it reflect the reality of the police force, where there are fewer women officers?

Content analysis as part of media research requires many of hours of scrutinising media output and logging the findings. You can carry out your own small-scale analysis over a couple of evenings of viewing or by looking at half a dozen issues of a newspaper or magazine.

Stereotypes

If a certain sort of person is represented in a similar way over and over again by the media, what is called a 'stereotype' of that kind of person develops. A stereotype is a fixed idea about the characteristics of a certain type of person or thing. Many characters in fairy-tales and pantomimes are stereotypes; the audience recognises them instantly and believes that they act in certain ways and have certain characteristics. For example, if a woman dressed in black with a pointed hat and a broomstick appears in a pantomime, the audience immediately assumes she is an evil witch and will hiss and boo to show disapproval. A similar process is at work when an old person is portrayed as grumpy or senile in a television soap opera. Other stereotypes include fat people being shown as funny, successful businesswomen as unemotional, and people who live in the country as less intelligent than those who live in cities.

> "Instead of being presented with stereotypes... children must have the opportunity to learn that within each range, some people are loathsome and some are delightful." **Margaret Mead**

Comedy programmes like Little Britain *use stereotypes to create humour*

Media stereotypes of some groups have been seen as particularly offensive. It is argued that they increase prejudice in society. This is often true of the representation of people from ethnic-minority backgrounds, homosexuals and members of certain religious groups. In extreme cases, the media can be used to encourage violence against certain groups. This happened in Nazi Germany, where Jews were the subject of vicious and twisted propaganda.

Stereotyping has a number of clear dangers. As you can see from the above example, stereotyping whole groups of people can end up in them being marginalised within our society. That means that because media representations of people encourage us to laugh at them or despise them, they are pushed to the edges of our society and have little power or influence. This was true of gay people for many years. Media representations and social attitudes meant that being gay was something people were made to feel ashamed of. As some minority groups like gay people gain acceptance within society, negative representations seem to be thrust upon other minorities. For example, asylum seekers and economic migrants are often represented negatively by the media, which can lead to public distrust of these groups. This is sometimes called the ideological work of the media, which means that the media influence the values and beliefs in our society.

Are you a stereotype?

Perhaps some of the strongest stereotypes portrayed in the media are those of young people. One that is easily recognisable is the youngster from a so called 'broken home' who gets into trouble with the police. This portrayal has become so common that it is almost taken for granted that in TV programmes any teenager who breaks the law must have family problems. This stereotype ignores those young people from stable family backgrounds who get into trouble, and law-abiding teenagers from single-parent homes.

One of the major factors that helps build up a stereotype is the way people in the media dress. Whenever a young person is portrayed as being on the slippery slope to a life of a drugs and crime, they are almost certain to be dressed in a way that goes against adult ideas about sensible clothes. If a teenage character in a TV programme is going off the rails, this is not signalled by the character going out and getting a smart haircut and an outfit suitable for an interview; the character is more likely to be dressed in the latest street fashion. Similarly pop bands tend to use their clothes to present a rebellious image in order to attract fans. Once they are famous, their fans may well adopt the dress style of the band, helping to make the stereotype stronger.

The use of clothes to represent youthful rebellion has affected the way young people are perceived. Look at the picture below. It shows a young man in trendy clothes going through the bag of an old lady. Has he mugged her? Or perhaps the old lady suffers from a heart condition, or asthma, and has asked the man to get her medication from her handbag. Your view of what is going on is determined to a large degree by a stereotype presented to you by the media.

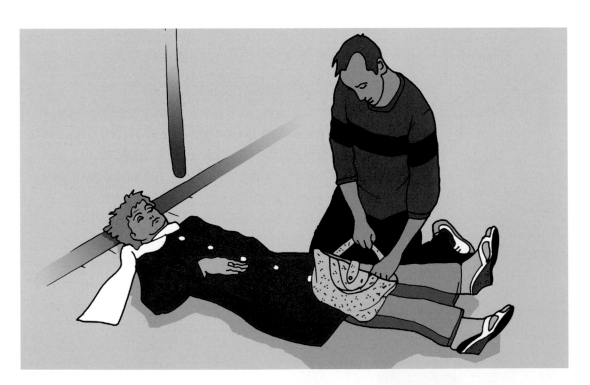

Some young people are stereotyped by the fact that they are hardly ever represented in the media. Young people with disabilities are rarely shown in films or on television. If they do appear, they are shown only to highlight the issue of disability, rather than as characters in their own right.

REVIEW

Representation is the key function of the media. You should, however, always ask yourself the following questions:

- Whose representation is it?
- What reason could the media have for representing the person, group, issue or event in this way?
- How else could the person, group, issue or event be represented?
- What is the effect of representing them in this way?

4 Institutions

Imagine you wake up one day and decide to publish your own newspaper, or to make a new quiz show for Channel 4, or to set up a community radio station. The chances are that no matter how enthusiastic you are about your schemes, they are unlikely to get very far – at least not in the short term. This is because however talented or hardworking you may be, in order to do any of these things you will need access to technology and money to pay for the resources to get your idea off the ground. You will need these things because you are going to make a product or commodity that you want people to use, in just the same way that any other manufacturer makes a product to be sold.

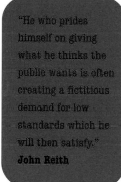

> "He who prides himself on giving what he thinks the public wants is often creating a fictitious demand for low standards which he will then satisfy."
> **John Reith**

Of course, you may be very rich, in which case your dreams could become a reality. Even so, there is no guarantee that your newspaper, quiz show or radio station would be a success and pay back the money invested in it. Media institutions are big business. They exist to make a profit. Just as car manufacturers or supermarket chains aim to earn money for their shareholders, so media institutions are owned by people who want them to make as much money as possible.

There are, of course, exceptions. For example, the BBC is funded through a licence fee, which everyone in the UK who uses a television has to pay. Even so, the BBC is expected to help fund itself through, for instance, the sales of programmes overseas and the publication of spin-off books and magazines.

Bush House, the original headquarters of the BBC, now the home of the BBC World Service

The BBC is often quoted as an example of an institution which is responsible for public service broadcasting. While other radio and television companies have obligations to public service broadcasting, because of its public funding, the BBC is most in the spotlight over its public service responsibilities.

The idea behind public service is that an institution is expected to provide a quality service to meet the widely different needs of the many audiences which will tune in. The BBC's first Director General in 1922, John Reith, set its goals as being to "educate, inform and entertain". The present day BBC is often criticised for having become too concerned with entertainment at the expense of education and information. People cite the number of make-over programmes that have been screened, for example. The BBC, on the other hand, would point to its vast investment in digital technology to ensure audiences are offered a variety of programming appropriate to all tastes, including BBC4, which provides quality programmes to quite small audiences.

Types of institution

Multinationals

A car manufacturer has to invest money in land, buildings and equipment in order to make cars. In the same way, a media producer has to pay or rent such items as TV studios, printing presses or transmitters in order to deliver its product to the consumer. Car manufacturers maximise their profit by producing cars that are sold all over the world. Such firms with world-wide interests are called multinationals. Many media institutions are also multinationals, with interests in a wide range of media and cultural products. This book, for example, is produced by Collins Educational, which is part of the international company HarperCollins Publishers. HarperCollins is in turn owned by News International, Rupert Murdoch's vast media empire. Other media interests that are part of News International include *The Sun* and *The Times* newspapers, and Sky Television, as well as other media industries across the globe.

The process by which media organisations become large companies controlling media output throughout countries across the world is known as globalisation. There is a lot to be gained for a large television company or a Hollywood studio to have access to global markets. At a simple level it means that they can sell their product to more people and make a better return on the money they have invested in a television programme or film. Globalisation is important because large multinational companies are usually based in western countries such as the USA and the United Kingdom. Not only do they maximise their profits by exporting their products, they also export western influence and even control over other cultures, especially those in developing countries. Many people would argue that this can have a harmful effect on these cultures and that exporting a western lifestyle to them is not necessarily in their best interests.

Such control of media output in the hands of one organisation, and ultimately one person, is a cause of great concern to many people.

The Sun, for instance, has a circulation of four million daily and is read by one in four of the population in the UK. It is so influential in swaying political opinion in the UK that it has arguably decided the outcome of general elections. Many people feel that ownership of the media has become unequal, especially where such corporations as News International control a variety of different media across the world. Too much power, they argue, is in the hands of too few people (see the section on controlling institutions on pages 62–63).

Small institutions

Small institutions are at the opposite end of the spectrum to the multinational media corporations. They may use limited technology to produce alternate or community-based media products. Football supporters, for example, may buy a copy of a fanzine written by other fans of the same club. Such fanzines exist outside the established media and may offer more radical points of view. Music fans produce fanzines offering a different perspective on the music scene or on a specific type of music. In some cases, they become part of the mainstream of media institutions. *When Saturday Comes* started as a small-circulation fanzine but is now on sale throughout the country.

> "The world is changing very fast. Big will not beat small anymore. It will be the fast beating the slow."
> **Rupert Murdoch**

Both the Arctic Monkeys and Sandi Thom benefited from internet promotion of their first singles

In the 1960s popular music was not well catered for by mainstream radio. Several pirate stations sprang up to fill the gap. These were sometimes housed on boats anchored off the coast just outside the control of the authorities. This practice went on until 1967, when the BBC launched Radio 1. Many of the presenters who had worked for these pirate stations were given shows on the new legitimate radio service.

Increasing use of the internet has significantly changed the way in which many alternative media organisations operate. Rather than go to all the trouble of printing a magazine to reach an audience of a few hundred people, organisations can now create a website with a potential audience of millions. Potentially anyone with a fairly basic knowledge of information and computer technology can build a site and become a media institution.

51

A good example of the power of the internet is the rise of the Sheffield band The Arctic Monkeys. By allowing fans to download demo tracks via the web, the band built up a following based on their own direct contact with their fans rather than through the marketing department of a record company. This opportunity to take action and promote music directly empowers artists and bands because fans judge them through their music rather than by the image that has been created by the record company. (See also the section on music downloads on page 166.)

> "If you can generate energy, it will eventually translate into business. MySpace is in the forefront of shifting the idea of what is worth money. It's just the beginning."
> **Billy Corgan**

This opportunity of the individual to make their voice heard through new media technology is not limited to bands promoting themselves and their music. Technology now allows people to communicate their ideas and opinions in ways that could not have been imagined in the last century. One example is internet bulletin boards and discussion groups, which people have been able to contribute their ideas to for some time now. These are virtual communities of people with shared interests who use webspace to share and exchange ideas and information. On a more individual basis, new media technology allows people opportunities to express their ideas through such innovations as blogs, podcasts and vlogs.

A blog, short for weblog, is a site controlled by an individual in which they post information, ideas and opinions for other people to read. Blogs are usually based around a particular topic, such as politics, but some blogs take the form of an online diary. A blog can consist of words, images and links to other websites or blogs. They also present the opportunity for readers to give feedback to the blogger, but are different from newsgroups in that the blogger retains control over the topics covered.

> "In the future, everyone will be famous for fifteen people."
> **Momus**

The podcast is a development of the blog. It relies on the ability of people to download audio and video files to portable listening devices such as iPods. Podcasting is derived from the words 'iPod' and 'broadcast'. Podcasts allow people to search the web to find material that they feel will be interesting and download it for listening or viewing later. One of the best-known examples of a podcast is *The Ricky Gervais Show*, which can be downloaded from the Guardian Unlimited

The websites MySpace and YouTube allow users to network directly with others who share their tastes and interests

website. After the success of his comedy series *The Office*, Ricky Gervais made the conscious decision to use this technology. He argued that instead of broadcasting to a mass audience he wanted to broadcast to an audience of people who would seek his comedy show and make the effort to get access to it.

A vlog, or video log, as its name suggests, is a blog in which the primary content is video material. This form of communication has become more popular as people unlock the potential of the video capabilities on their mobile phones to record material which they can then upload to their vlog site. This is sometimes called a moblog.

All three of these technologies have enabled people to short circuit the process of getting their ideas heard by using existing mass media institutions and have allowed them direct access to audiences. This is particularly important to people who feel they are living in regimes where their freedom of speech is being repressed or simply to those who find it hard to get their voice heard through traditional media channels.

Another important area of growth is the availability of online television stations. Although these are mostly existing stations which are made available through the internet using broadband connections to stream them to viewers, the technology has the potential to let people set up their own television station. Of course, this technology is at an early stage and it is not clear to what extent an individual might seriously be able to develop and sustain their own broadcasting setup.

Value systems

Media institutions have so far been discussed in terms of being organisations made up of equipment, bricks and mortar. The word 'institution' carries with it another important connotation, though. The place where you are taking your Media Studies course is probably an institution. It is not simply a series of buildings in which people attend lessons, but a system of values and conventions by which people work and study together. Some of these conventions are written down, for instance, rules about smoking. Some conventions exist because people agree that they should, or because they have always existed. Most will make sense to everyone, while others will seem silly to some people.

A media institution will carry with it a similar value system, supported by conventions concerning the way things should be done. You sometimes hear it called 'professionalism', which implies that this is the way that people who are good at the job will do it. Professionalism means sticking to the standards and work practices that are the norm within a particular industry or institution. What makes a good news story is a matter of professional judgement. Which news story is the most important is another matter of professional judgement. In television news, presenters are always smartly dressed and speak directly and clearly to the audience in 'proper' English – they are professional.

These notions of professionalism, or the right way to do things, exist in all media. There is a 'right' way to write newspaper stories, take news photographs or introduce records on the radio. These are part of the conventions that were discussed in Chapter 2, on the language used by the media. Anyone who gets a job in a media institution will be expected to adopt the same attitudes and approaches to the job as those who already work there. In fact, some people argue that recruitment into the media is limited to people of fairly restricted backgrounds. Others argue that this is changing. Certainly organisations, such as the BBC, have equal opportunities policies designed to ensure that people from under-represented minorities are positively encouraged to apply for jobs.

Professional working practices can make anything that is different from them seem amateur. If you look at one of your own attempts at practical production, you will probably compare it to a professional production and feel a little disappointed. It is difficult to produce anything that you can feel proud of if its value is going to be measured against the work of experienced professionals with vast resources at their disposal.

If you look at home-produced fanzines or listen to a pirate radio, however, it becomes clear that some people are not simply trying, and failing, to imitate what the professionals do. These alternative media may, in fact, have been created because the major media institutions themselves have failed to address the issues that the audience feel are relevant. Of course, the irony is that if the alternative media are too successful, they themselves will be swallowed into the mainstream and become part of the system they were opposing.

Taking risks

Supposed you manage to find the money to set yourself up as a media institution. Many people would be quick to tell you that the media is a good place to lose your money. Your investment, as it is called, would be quite risky. This is one of the arguments that multinational media companies put forward in defence of their large and diverse interests. By spreading their risks over a wide range of different products, they stand less chance of losing out completely if they don't get it right.

The problem for media producers is the unpredictability of the audience. For example, most media products are designed to be consumed over a short period of time. The consumer who buys a car or a pair of socks will enjoy these products over a relatively long period of time, which makes them seem good value for money. A film, on the other hand, lasts for only a couple of hours, and consumers judge it on the pleasure they get during that time. This makes the success of a film difficult to predict. Even products that can give more lengthy enjoyment, such as magazines, rely heavily on an immediate appeal and impact on the reader.

Unlike a car or a sock, a media product is rarely a standard item that can be mass-produced. Each television programme has to be different from every other television programme. But, as pointed out in Chapter 2, pages 8–33, it will probably contain many similarities with others of its genre. Media producers have to tread a very careful path between identifying and repeating a successful formula, and producing new and innovative products. If they get it wrong, their investment will probably turn into a loss.

Audiences may choose to see a film just on the strength of the stars appearing in it. L to R: Catherine Zeta Jones, George Clooney, Brad Pitt, Nicole Kidman

Media producers are, however, able to take steps to cut the risk factor to a minimum. On television, one-off pilot programmes are often made to try out a formula before a full series of programmes is made. The pilots will be tested on the market, and only if audiences respond positively will a studio commit money to the full project.

Working with an established and successful genre is one means of reducing the risk. Another is to use well-known stars. This is especially true in the case of Hollywood films, where a star name is a big box-office draw and is likely to provide some guarantee

of a film's popularity. Similarly, in the music industry recording companies prefer to invest money in promoting stars who are already established, rather than risking it on new or up-and-coming talent. In fact, the media industry relies heavily on the concept of celebrity. The famous (and not-so-famous) fill the pages of newspapers and magazines, and appear on countless TV chat shows and radio programmes. Some celebrities are even said to be famous just for being famous!

Despite all efforts by the big institutions to make sure that they invest in winning formulas, the media is littered with products that audiences did not want, many of them quite spectacular failures. Each of these products represents an instance of a media producer who failed to guess correctly what the audience wanted.

Competition between institutions

Market segmentation

In recent years, institutions have brought about an increasing segmentation of markets in their desire to sell to audiences (see Chapter 5, page 71–72). Market segmentation is the breaking down of the market for media products into small units. For example, within the magazine market, specialist magazines with a limited audience – and therefore a small circulation – can be said to have segmented the market. Instead of selling large amounts of a product that appeals to a mass audience, institutions sell products to much more specialised audiences. Changes in working practices and technology have made printing cheaper, which means that magazines that can be profitable with just a small circulation. In fact, many small ventures are owned by large media institutions. Quite often rival titles on magazine racks are owned by the same company.

The growth of satellite and cable broadcasting with their use of digital technology has led to increasing segmentation in the television market. In urban areas especially, increasing numbers of viewers receive a package of programmes through their local cable operator. The cable operator downloads many of the programmes via satellite and feeds them by means of fibre-optic cable to individual homes. Many, however, still rely on a satellite dish to receive programmes. These receive a signal bounced off a satellite. A signal is fed from the dish to a combined receiver-decoder, which is able to unscramble the encrypted signal with the help of a smart card supplied to the subscribers. Programmes can then be received on a TV set and recorded on DVD or hard disk recorder, in the same way as is possible with a terrestrial channel. The advent of digital technologies means that there has been an increase in the number of different channels available; it also means that programmes are even more able to cater for niche markets of audiences with specialised interests. For example, channels aimed at people who like music are now segmented into more specific genres of music, such as pop, dance, hip-hop and indie. News and entertainment targeted at Asian viewers is available through the Star channels, offering Bollywood films and an Indian news channel.

Digital technology has also led to a rise in 'pay per view' programming. This means that subscribers can pay an additional sum of money to watch a specific programme. Commonly this is a major sporting event, broadcast live, or a recently released film. Many people dislike the fact that these 'special' programmes are available only to those with the technology and who are able to pay. They argue that the free public-service channel can only offer less important and less attractive events, as the subscription-based channels outbid them for the rights to screen the major events.

Subscribers to Sky TV film packages can also download films direct to their computers where they can be stored on hard disk for viewing at a convenient time. This is a good example of convergence technology. Convergence is the coming together of digital technologies, in this case broadband technology and television, to offer audiences greater freedom and control over what they watch and when they watch it. Increasingly technology will be sold with this capacity for linking broadband access with the traditional television receiver, which will also provide higher levels of interactivity to allow audiences to vote and even buy goods they see advertised. The computer screen and the television screen are likely soon to become one.

Digital technology is also becoming more accessible for radio broadcasting. This is likely to have a similar effect to the one it has had on TV, increasing the choice of stations available to audiences and creating niche markets targeted at those with specific tastes and interests. (See Chapter 11.)

Marketing the product

When a big car company launches a new model, most people get to know about it. Television, press and radio advertising, features in motoring supplements, billboard adverts and displays in car dealers' showrooms announce and promote the new product. Similarly, the media industries have their own marketing ploys for ensuring that a product is likely to reach the audience at which it is aimed.

On TV we are constantly bombarded with trailers for programmes that will be shown later that night, that week or even that month. Continuity announcers tell the audience between programmes about other media institutions, and television listings appear in all the national dailies. Television news magazines tell us what the papers say. Radio programmes discuss what is on television that night, or what you missed last night. Programmes such as soap operas, and reality TV such as *Big Brother*, regularly feature in the popular press as their stars become engaged in headline-grabbing scandals.

Scheduling

Of course, despite common ownership, real competition exists between media institutions. Each one wants to obtain the largest share of the market so that it can charge advertisers large sums of money for the privilege of promoting their products. Even an institution like the BBC needs to attract large audiences for its programmes, despite its commitment to public service broadcasting.

This competition for audiences can be seen across the media. For example, in the press, *The Sun* and the *Daily Mirror* are involved in so-called 'tabloid wars', a battle for the largest circulation. In fact, newspapers in general take extreme measures to try to maintain their circulation in what is generally a dwindling market. The offer of a free CD or DVD is a common marketing ploy to encourage readers to buy a copy of a newspaper, be it a popular title or a quality one. In our case study on radio (see pages 202–219), we study the competition between public service and commercial broadcasting. The style-magazine market is another circulation battleground, with magazines competing for the prize of advertising revenue for products aimed at the stylish under-thirties.

The most obvious example of competition between media institutions is the battle for prime-time viewing audiences. This fight is mainly between BBC1 and ITV, with increasing competition from the satellite channels. Each channel wants to maximise the viewing audience for its prime-time slots. Early evening programming is very important to 'hook' the audience into watching a particular channel in the hope that they will stay with it throughout the evening. Australian soaps, popular especially with younger viewers, are scheduled in prime early evening slots to grab the audience in preparation for programming later that evening.

Drive-time is an important concept in radio listening. Drivers on their way to or from work tune in for news and travel information, as well as for the companionship that the radio provides on a journey. Modern car radios can be programmed to retune automatically to the station that is giving out travel information or a news bulletin, even if the driver is listening to a CD at the time.

Television news programmes are an important part of an evening's scheduling. BBC1 and ITV used to schedule their main evening news to avoid clashing head to head with one another. Now they broadcast the news at the same time in direct competition. Both channels clearly like to have a fixed time slot for the news. In consequence, they have to schedule other programmes around these slots, which form a key element in shaping an evening's viewing for many family audiences.

Some commentators have made the important point that because news is part of an evening's entertainment, this has an effect on the way in which it is presented. While the news should inform, it must hold the attention of the viewer in competition with programmes that are made to entertain or amuse. In other words, the news is under pressure to compete with other programmes.

Another important aspect of scheduling is what broadcasters call the 'nine o'clock watershed'. This means the time after which more adult content – swearing, violence and sex – can be included in programmes, because (at least in theory) younger viewers for whom such material is deemed unsuitable will probably be in bed. In other words, scheduling is used to maximise a channel's audience, but there are factors that restrict the schedule. (The ways in which material is regulated are discussed in more detail in Chapter 5, pages 64–87.)

Not all programmes are aimed at a mass audience. On television, BBC2 and Channel 4 were both deliberately set up to attract minority audiences who were not well catered for by the mainstream channels. Ratings are generally much smaller. Snooker on BBC2, for example, and to a lesser extent racing on Channel 4 are examples of popular programmes attracting audiences who might otherwise be unaware of these channels and what they offer. Even minority-interest channels have to take account of the need to attract sizeable audiences.

Babyshambles lead singer Pete Doherty dodges the press outside Thames Magistrate Court in London

Controlling institutions

It has been argued that in a democratic society we should have a media that is free from control and able to express opinions as it wishes, without interference from government. Other people argue that some elements of the media abuse that freedom and behave irresponsibly, for example, by invading people's privacy, taking photographs when they are off guard.

The media is subject to a range of different regulations. Some of these are statutory, which means that they have the force of law behind them. Libel is an example of a statutory regulation. If a newspaper or news bulletin says something that is defamatory, or harmful to someone's reputation, that person can take legal action to sue the newspaper or programme for the damage they have done. Another example of control over what the media does is called self-regulation. This means that the industry itself punishes those who go beyond the bounds of what is acceptable. An example of self-regulation is the Press Complaints Commission (PCC), which deals with complaints about the newspaper industry. The work of the PCC is considered in more detail in Chapter 8 (pages 126–161). Most sections of the media industry are controlled in some way by regulatory bodies, such as the Independent Television Commission (ITC), which have varying powers to control what the media can and cannot do. These bodies are looked at in more detail in Chapter 5 (pages 64–87.

Governments throughout the world have an interest in who controls the flow of information. For many governments, controlling the media is an effective way of stifling the voices of people who do not agree with them. In many countries there is censorship of the media, which means that the government decides what can and cannot be published or broadcast.

One method of international mass communication poses a real threat to efforts to control the information that passes between people across the globe – the internet. This was originally set up as a means of communication in the event of nuclear war, so that survivors throughout the world could communicate by computer. Because it crosses international boundaries and is made up largely of contributions from individuals, it is hard to police. Already the USA and several other countries have introduced legislation to control what people put on the internet. They argue that it is important to control access to material that is indecent or pornographic.

As we have seen, however, the internet does allow ordinary people the opportunity to make their voices heard. Many argue that as the media is increasingly controlled by large multinational organisations, it is becoming more and more difficult for individuals with different points of view to get these across. By resisting attempts to control the internet, they argue that they are fighting to preserve their freedom to express ideas without government interference.

REVIEW

Institutions are important because you need money, equipment and resources to create media products. Media institutions may be multi-national or quite small, commercial or publicly funded like the BBC. They often compete with one another for a share of the market. What media institutions can do and say is controlled both by the law and by regulatory bodies.

5 Audience

Audience is the word used to describe people who consume media products. This includes viewers of television programmes, cinema-goers, radio listeners and readers of newspapers, magazines and comics. The importance of audience to the media is obvious. All the papers, broadcasts and recordings in the world would mean nothing if no one read, watched or listened to them. Without an audience, the media would be talking to itself. A question often asked in Media Studies, though, is 'Who is in control?' Does the media control the audience, or the audience control the media?

The media's effects on its audience

The evil empire

On one side of the debate are those who argue that the media is a very powerful force and that the effects it has on its audiences are largely bad. They believe that people, especially those who are easily influenced, tend to imitate what they see or read. There are many violent and sexual images in the media, which they say lead to more irresponsible behaviour in society. Some people have also claimed that the portrayal of some types of behaviour on television has led to a decline in what are called 'moral standards'. They say that young people have copied the behaviour of characters in television dramas and that this has created a society in which people have lost respect for one another.

"I would say to Radio 1, do you realise that some of the stuff you play on Saturday nights encourages people to carry guns and knives?" **David Cameron**

Similar concerns have been expressed about the lyrics in popular music. Artists such as Eminem are said to have a bad influence on their young audiences because of the language they use and the attitudes they express in their songs. Some parents fear their children will adopt both the language and attitudes they hear. Others see the issue as being rather more complicated. They argue that most people do not go out and do things simply because they have seen them portrayed in the media or because their idol, or role model, behaves in a certain way. Indeed, part of the attraction of listening to rap artists is arguably nothing more sinister than that it annoys or worries one's parents.

The rap artist Eminem

It can also be argued that the media is a positive force in our society. It has an important educational function, informing people not only about what is going on in the world but also helping them live healthier and more fulfilling lives. It also makes an important contribution to our culture, with people from all walks of life given access to a wide range of films, drama, music and even high-brow events such as ballet and opera.

65

"There are more love songs than anything else. If songs could make you do something we'd all love one another." **Frank Zappa**

The argument surrounding the way in which the media influences our lives is called the 'effects debate'. No one knows for certain how the media does influence its audiences. What is clear is that the relationship is a complex one and that we should be wary of making simple judgements about how the media might impact upon people's behaviour.

Concern in Britain in the 1960s over the content of films and programmes on TV and radio led in 1965 to the creation of the National Viewers' and Listeners' Association. Its founder, Mary Whitehouse, became a national figure through her campaigns to clean up British television. The concerns expressed also led to what is known as the 'nine o'clock watershed' on terrestrial channels. This is an agreement not to show explicit sex or violence before 9 pm, so that parents know that they can let their children watch programmes before this time.

Newspapers and magazines have not escaped criticism. Explicit photography and the detailed descriptions of sex and violence in newspapers are believed by some to have a negative influence on readers. Magazines aimed at teenagers have been attacked for promoting sexual promiscuity by publishing material on contraception and physical relationships. Music, fashion and gossip magazines have been slated for their 'glorification' of the bad behaviour of celebrities and stars. Programmes such as *The X Factor* have been accused of misleading people into believing that even with very little natural talent or any real effort they can become an overnight success by being 'discovered'.

The power of the media to influence, if not offend, is officially recognised by regulatory bodies set up to keep an eye on media output. The British Board of Film Classification (BBFC) gives each film and video a certificate stating whether it is suitable for children or young people to watch. The BBFC can also decide that a film or video is not suitable for public distribution and refuse to give it a certificate. All films and videos have to be certified by the BBFC if they are to be distributed legally to the public in Britain, although local councils have the final decision on whether a film should be shown in cinemas in their area. The BBFC started life as the British Board of Film Censors in 1912, set up to advise local councils on which films were suitable for public viewing. It became known as the British Board of Film Classification in 1985 when it was designated under the Video Recording Act 1984 as the organisation that would carry out the classification of videos for sale or rent.

The BBFC classification symbols usually appear on videos and DVDs, although sometimes you also find them on posters advertising films. Each film receives a certificate that states its category, which must be displayed before the film begins. 'Uc' is a category specially invented for videos. Videos that are exempt from classification are usually labelled 'E'; this applies to music and educational videos, for example.

Television has been blamed for a range of social ills, from sexual promiscuity to childhood obesity

Consumer advice is also found on videos and DVDs. It is in a form laid down by the BBFC. So you may find information on a film you are going to rent or buy that advises you what to expect. For example, it may contain 'moderate violence', 'strong sex' or 'hard drugs references'. In this way audiences, particularly parents of young children, are able to make considered decisions about the content of a video or DVD before they buy or rent it.

Video and computer games present new problems of classification. Many games are violent and use realistic graphics. Digital technology has developed CD-ROMs (Compact Disc Read Only Memory), CD-I (Compact Disc-interactive) and DVD (Digital Versatile Discs). These formats allow video images, including those showing extreme violence and explicit sex, to be stored on disc and played on computers. Some material of this sort is controlled under the Video Recordings Act (1984), and the BBFC is responsible for assessing it, via its video classification system. Many video and computer games, however, are exempt because they do not contain significant violence, sex and criminal techniques. In an attempt to deal with this situation, the computer games industry has designed its own voluntary system of categories for games not covered by the Video Recordings Act.

In 2003 a regulatory body called Ofcom, or the Office of Communications, was formed. This body is responsible for the regulation of all broadcast output in the United Kingdom as well as for looking after telecommunications and wireless communications, which covers such things as the mobile phone networks. A prime function of Ofcom is to regulate against the broadcasting of offensive material on television and radio. Ofcom does, however, have other more positive functions. It is responsible for 'ensuring a wide range of TV and radio services of high quality and wide appeal,' which means that it is Ofco's job to see that we get good quality programmes that offer something to all sectors of the audience.

British Board of Film Classification certification		
Film	**Symbol**	**Video**
Universal: suitable for viewers of all ages	**U**	Universal: suitable for all
	Uc	Particularly suitable for young children
Parental Guidance: whether children should watch the film is left for parents to decide	**PG**	Parental Guidance: suitable for general viewing, but some scenes may be unsuitable for younger children
Suitable only for viewers of 12 years and over	**12**	Suitable only for persons of 12 years and over. Not to be supplied to any person below that age
Suitable only for viewers of 15 years and older	**15**	Suitable only for persons of 15 years and over. Not to be supplied to any person below that age
Suitable only for viewers of 18 years and older. Contains scenes or language of an adult nature that are unsuitable for viewers under the age of 18	**18**	Suitable only for persons of 18 years and over. Not to be supplied to any person below that age
For restricted distibution only. To be viewed only at cinemas to which no one under the age of 18 is admitted	**R18** RESTRICTED	For restricted distibution only. To be supplied only in licensed sex shops to persons of not less than 18 years

Brainwashing buyers

It is advertising that has provoked perhaps the most repeated attacks on the media's effect on audiences. Advertising is one of the major ways in which media producers make money. Manufacturers pay the media to promote images of their products, which they hope will encourage people to buy them. Many people say that the media's most important function is not to entertain audiences, but to deliver customers to advertisers. An enormous amount of advertising is carried in the media. Up to 60% of a newspaper's content is made up of advertisements. On commercial television, adverts appear an average four times an hour. On radio stations, too, they are played frequently.

Even the non-commercial BBC broadcasts advertisements for its own merchandise, such as videos and books associated with its programmes.

Critics say that the way audiences are bombarded with advertising is little short of brainwashing. They believe that the sophisticated promotion of products in the media must lead viewers and listeners to buy things they don't need. The powerful effect of advertising on children causes particular disagreement and discussion. Parents complain about adverts for toys being shown during and around children's TV programmes. They say that advertisers know that children will pester their parents to buy the toys they have seen advertised on television. More recently a lot of concern has been voiced about the way in which foods high in fat and sugar are advertised to children. Given that obesity is an issue for many young children today, it is argued that advertising unhealthy foods puts both children and their parents under unnecessary pressure to consume foods that may be doing them harm.

> "In general my children refuse to eat anything that hasn't danced on television."
> **Erma Bombeck**

Children are not alone, however, in being deemed open to the effects of advertising. Success with the opposite sex, luxurious lifestyles, ultimate happiness and freedom from worry are all promised by advertisements, for everything from chocolate to floor polish. The Advertising Standards Authority regulates the content of adverts in the media by monitoring such factors as taste, honesty and decency. (See Chapter 10, pages 186–201.)

Television and computer zombies

The media has been accused of having an even more sinister effect on its audience; it has been charged with turning people into virtual zombies, addicted to the glow of television and computer screens. A frightening picture is painted of people whose minds have been hijacked by the media. Children are seen as glued to the TV set instead of playing creatively. Teenagers are portrayed as living in a fantasy world of computer games. Adults are shown as being concerned only with soap operas, newspaper gossip and the latest product advertised on television. The media is charged with the break-up of family life, as adults gather round the television and children are hypnotised by the computer screen. This picture of the media's effect is known as the

Lara Croft, heroine of the bestselling Tomb Raider *series*

'hypodermic model'. The idea is that the media injects its consumers with the message and meanings it chooses and that the audience has no real power to resist. In support of this argument, it is pointed out that many people actually believe that what they see in soap operas is real. When a popular character dies, it is common for wreaths to be sent to the studio by grief stricken viewers. It is also noted that a good deal of space, especially in popular newspapers, is taken up with the news from soap operas, rather than from the real world.

> "Television is designed to brainwash us all and the internet to eliminate any last resistance." **Paul Carvel**

Others believe, however, that this model seriously oversimplifies the complex relationship between media audiences and media texts. Yet evidence seems to exist that we should be concerned about the media having an effect on our behaviour. Advertising, for example, seeks to persuade audiences – with some success – to consume certain products. Indeed, the power of advertising is considered so great that some products, such as cigarettes, cannot be advertised on television.

Audience segmentation

It is important neither to overestimate the power of the audience nor to underestimate the ability of the media to take advantage of the audience's demands. Increasingly, media producers are cleverly identifying and splitting off ('segmenting') particular audiences in order to make money. Satellite and cable TV companies have been particularly good at this. If you look at the satellite and cable listings in any magazines you will see a host of channels aimed at minority or 'niche' markets. These will include pop music, sports, and specialist film and documentary channels. Such channels are clearly designed to appeal to special interest groups. This allows advertisers to target audiences very precisely with goods and services that are likely to interest them.

Many researchers into the way in which audiences relate to the media feel that a fundamental change is taking place in the way in which people use and access media products. Much of this change is driven by advances in technology, particularly the arrival of digital technology. This has allowed audiences much greater freedom and choice in their consumption of the media. Audiences are said to have become more active. This can be seen in a number of ways. Firstly access to the internet, particularly through high-speed broadband connections, has made the downloading of media products such as music and films much more widely available. The fact that many of these products can be loaded on to personal communication devices such as iPods means that audiences can carry them about and consume them when they wish. No longer do they have to assemble in front of the television in the lounge at a scheduled time if they are to catch a programme.

Many critics feel that this segmentation of audiences is likely to increase as technology allows people to demand more and more of what they want to see, when they want to see it. Many people believe we are currently witnessing the end of the era of mass audiences, when millions of people all watch the same programme networked on national television. Instead we will use technology to demand the programme we want to watch when it is most convenient to us, and by the means most convenient to us.

Audience participation

One method the media has used to increase consumption of its products is audience participation. This means getting the audience involved in the media itself. Some television programmes depend on the audience providing most of the entertainment. These include shows made up of home videos sent in by viewers, or amateur talent contests, where, for example, people are auditioned by singing down the telephone or sending in a video of their dance talents.

Big Brother *housemate Jade Goody went on to establish a successful career in the media*

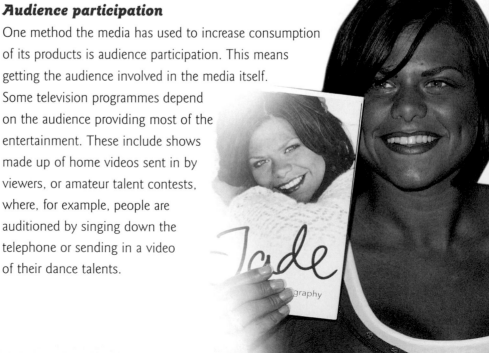

More recent – and popular – forms of audience participation are docu-soaps and reality TV. Programmes such as *Big Brother* and *Extreme Makeover* feature ordinary members of the public and in effect turn the audience into the stars of the show. The popularity of such shows has encouraged media producers to develop new series and to create other shows in the same genre. The appetite of the tabloid press for stories about the 'stars' seems insatiable. Many of the people featured in these shows fade back into the obscurity from which they emerged. Others, such as Jade Goody, build show-business careers on the strength of their original appearance. Reality TV is discussed further in Chapter 13.

One area in which audience participation in the media has increased significantly is in news and current affairs programming. The use of websites, email, texting and telephone services has meant that audiences can respond quickly to issues that are raised as part of news broadcasts and similar topical programmes. Indeed, broadcasters have become highly dependent on audience feedback as an important feature of programmes such as news bulletins, where the audience are asked to get in touch with the channel to express their views or even ask questions on a topic.

Survivors of the 2005 London bombings became 'citizen journalists' by using their mobile phones to film their escape

In addition, we also have the phenomenon of the 'citizen' or 'accidental' journalist. This name has been coined to describe people who witness news events first hand and use the video recorder on their mobile phone to record

footage of the event. They then make this available to news bulletins for broadcast. Such footage, although often technically poor compared to professional filming, has a dramatic first-hand quality which is obviously appealing to viewers. The bombings on the London Underground in July 2005 are a good example of 'accidental journalism', where survivors used mobile phones to film scenes of devastation and suffering as they escaped through the trains to safety.

The audience's effects on the media

Are you a radio addict, a TV slave or a computer zombie? Do you live in a fantasy world peopled by characters who don't really exist? When you see something advertised, do you feel you must go out and buy it? Your answer to these questions will probably be 'No'. The hypodermic model of the media's effect has been criticised for seeing audiences as too passive and stupid. After all, no one forces you to turn on the television or to buy a magazine. If the media was as much in control as the hypodermic model suggests, then people would watch, listen to or read anything that was broadcast or published; this is clearly not the case. Some television shows are unsuccessful, and newspapers and magazines go out of business. Not all products advertised in the media sell, and some bands heralded as the 'next big thing' flop. These are examples of the power exercised by audiences.

Another important way in which audiences interact with programmes is through voting to determine the outcome of shows. This happens across of a range of genres, but is particularly prevalent in reality television shows and talent contests. The direct feedback to the show via text, email and phone is used in these cases to determine whether people stay on the programme and win or are told to leave.

All this begs the question as to whose interests are being served by the opportunity presented to have a say in the media. There is an argument that this is another example of the 'democratisation' of the media, that ordinary people are being given the power to influence the content of media products and make important contributions. A more cynical view is that the real power remains with those who control what is included in, say, a television programme and that audience involvement is merely a cheap way of filling air time.

Audience power can be said to have led to the development of different forms of media. BBC Radio used to consist of just one station, the Home Service. This split into Radios 1, 2, 3 and 4 because it was recognised that there were different types of radio listeners; in other words, there were different audiences with distinct tastes.

On TV, Channel 4's early success was based on catering for so-called 'minority audiences' through programmes on subjects that were largely ignored by the BBC and mainstream television stations. Classic FM, a national commercial radio station that plays nothing but classical music, was launched after it was realised that there was an audience for it – a different audience from the one that listened to classical music on Radio 3. All these developments point to the power of the audience to affect what the media produces.

To get a clear picture of how the media works in our society, we must consider how audiences can actually influence what it produces. It may be that many people enjoy watching soap operas. It is not the case, however, that people will mindlessly watch any soap opera that is screened. The TV graveyard is full of soap operas that failed to attract enough viewers. Pressure from viewers can also lead programme makers to change scripts, kill off unpopular characters and even bring others back from the dead.

Finding out about the audience

How does the audience use the media?

In order to study audiences, it is important to consider how people actually use media products. People might watch soap operas for amusement, treating them more like pantomimes than dramas in which they become emotionally involved. Some people use the radio for companionship. They put it on to hear a friendly voice and are not too concerned which friendly voice it is. Teenagers might like a certain type of music because it is good to dance to, not because of its rebellious lyrics. People might buy a newspaper not to find out what is going on in the world but to check their horoscope, find out what is on television or simply look at the girl on page three.

This way of looking at the relationship between the media and its audience is called the 'uses and gratifications' approach. It considers how people use media

A scene from the cult American TV series CSI: Crime Scene Investigation

products and what they get out of them. They might use the media as part of their social lives. For example, going to the pictures can play a central role in the development of a relationship between two people. Friends might gather to watch a big match on television, or contact each other through requests or phone-ins on radio stations. For individuals, the media can provide a personal reflection of themselves in characters on TV. They may watch detective shows to test how good they are at working out 'whodunnit'. Or they may enjoy the tension of seeing whether characters become romantically involved in a drama.

The term 'uses and gratifications' suggests that instead of sitting around soaking up media messages in a passive way, audiences actively select their media consumption and use it for their own purposes. Rather than being used by the media, people are actually using it to obtain gratification, or pleasure, in a variety of different ways.

What does the audience want from the media?

Media producers need to know what people think about their products in order to increase the size of their audiences. To discover what is popular and what is not, media organisations do a great deal of audience research. Commercial audience research companies carry out these investigations for media producers. Additionally, organisations set up specifically to investigate audience include:

- **The Broadcasters Audience Research Board (BARB)**, which produces information on television audiences for the BBC and ITV television companies. This information includes the numbers of people watching programmes, their reactions to them and their reasons for watching them. BARB produces charts each week showing the 30 most-watched television programmes. Many newspapers publish charts showing the week's top 10 programmes, which are based on BARB's information. You can also look at the BARB website (www.barb.co.uk) to obtain up-to-date audience figures.
- **The Radio Joint Audience Research (RAJAR)**, which conducts research into radio audiences and the reasons why they tune in to particular stations and programmes.
- **The National Surveys Ltd (NRS)**, which calculates the number of people reading newspapers and magazines.

Audience research

To make sense of the information gathered through audience research, investigators group similar types of people into categories. This allows them to say which different kinds of people like or dislike particular media products. Measurements used to group people during research include age, sex, income, education and occupation. A very important measurement used in audience research is that of social class. A person's social class is determined by a combination of their income, education, lifestyle and other factors. Social classes in their broadest sense are split into upper, middle and lower or working classes. More complicated measurement scales split these three categories into smaller sections. The one used by many market research organisations is based on the Registrar General's scale of social class set out as long ago as 1911. Newspaper and magazine publishers use this scale to judge what percentage of their readers comes from which group. The scale separates people into six groups, depending on the job of the head of the household (or main wage-earner).

Audience Research Techniques

Asking people to keep diaries of what they listen to or watch

Interviews

Monitoring television sets to see which programmes are being watched

Questionnaires

Quantitative data or information in the form of numbers, such as how many people watched a particular programme or read a specific magazine.

Qualitative data or information on people's opinions about media products – whether they like them, for instance, and why or how they could be improved.

This profiling of audiences according to social background and disposable income has obvious limitations, particularly when advertisers are targeting audiences. A more up-to-date approach relies on the concept of psychographics devised by American advertising agency Young & Rubicam. Psychographics basically divides consumers by classifying them according to their attitudes and values.

The basic four categories can be described as:

- **Succeeders:** People who are successful and self-confident. They tend not to buy aspirational products and follow their own ideas of what is a good product.

A Commonly Used Class Description Scale	
Category	**Description**
A	Upper middle class
	People working in top-level management and professions
B	Middle class
	Middle-level managers and middle-ranking professionals
C1	Lower middle class
	Junior managers, supervisors, clerical workers, and lower-ranking professionals
C2	Skilled working class
	Skilled manual workers
D	Working class
	Semi-skilled and unskilled manual workers
E	People at lowest level income, for example, state pensioners and casual workers

- **Reformers:** Creative, caring (for example likely to be involved in charities), not brand conscious.
- **Aspirers:** People who want to 'get on'.
- **Mainstreamers:** The largest segment, conformists who buy 'safe', big brand products.

Audience positioning

One of the ways in which the media is believed to inject its powerful effect into audiences is through what is known as audience positioning. Audience positioning refers to the relationship between the audience and the media product. It also refers to how a media product addresses, or talks to, its audience. A media text offers a position to an audience in the way in which it lets them see the people, issues and events it covers.

As discussed in Chapter 3, media texts are not direct records of reality, but re-presentations' of it. Each media re-presentation is the product of a process of selection and editing of information, in the form of film shots, radio interviews or news stories. Because of this process, there will always be other possible re-presentations of the people, events, stories and issues appearing in the media. Crime dramas, for example, usually position the audience with the main detective character. The viewer follows the detective as if they were looking over his or her shoulder, gets the clues in the order the detective gets them, and sympathises with the detective's point of view. It is rare for a crime drama to position the audience with the criminal.

The position offered to audiences by media texts is not, however, the only possible one. Crime and police dramas could position the viewer with criminals, showing how they see the world and even encouraging viewers to sympathise with them. This does not usually happen, though. Why? Some say it is because it is in society's interests to promote 'good' behaviour and to discourage people from breaking the law. Others argue, however, that what is defined as 'good' behaviour is often biased. For example, people shown taking part in a demonstration in a police drama may be represented as nuisances, because the police may view them from the point of view of having to control such events. The right to demonstrate peacefully, though, is regarded as one of the basic rights of our society. The position offered to the audience in the police drama might therefore be seen as political, since it may influence viewers' opinions against the right to demonstrate.

Kiefer Sutherland in the hit American TV thriller 24

All media texts also have a way of talking to, or addressing, their users. The way a media text addresses its users also influences the position the user is offered. Television newsreaders address the viewer face to face, as if they were talking directly to them. They use a serious but sincere tone of voice, like that of a concerned friend. This, some argue, positions the viewer with the newsreader and encourages them to believe what he or she is saying. Remember, what the newsreader is saying is only a re-presentation of the news. However, because the newsreader appears to be friendly and worthy of trust, it is argued that viewers will tend to believe almost anything newsreaders say. This may be acceptable if news accounts are accurate, but what if they are biased or filled with lies?

Newspapers also position their readers through the way they address them. Stories in popular newspapers tend to be written as if the writer were having a conversation with the reader. It is assumed that the person reading the story will hold the same beliefs as those expressed in the paper. In fact, most popular newspapers claim that they do more than report the news: they say they speak for their readers. Most popular newspapers did not, for example, support striking miners during their long industrial dispute in 1984. Many printed appeals for an end to the strike. The position they offered their readers was firmly against the strikers and they addressed their readers as if they agreed with that position.

> "What TV is extremely good at – and realise that this is 'all it does' – is discerning what large numbers of people think they want, and supplying it." **David Foster Wallace**

Typical audiences

Most media producers have a typical viewer in mind when they are putting together their products. This is someone whom the media producers believe to be typical of the audience for a particular product. They mould these products to cater for the characteristics of the ideal consumer. For example, a men's lifestyle magazine may have a typical reader who is 35 years old, married with young children, works in an office, drives a car and takes foreign holidays. This is called an 'audience profile'. Most of the articles in the magazine will therefore be about topics that the publishers think a 35-year-old married man with children, a car and an office job will be interested in. This, then, will be the main audience position offered to the reader of the magazine.

In general, the presumed background and interests of the typical consumer will dictate the position given to the audience of a particular product. The audience position will determine such factors as:

- **The type of language used.** A children's TV programme will not use adult words that its audience might not understand. A presenter on a rock music programme will use the latest rock world slang, rather than the 'correct' English used on BBC Radio 4.
- **The tone of voice used.** Teenagers would be unlikely to watch or listen to television and radio programmes aimed at them if the presenters talked in dull, middle-aged voices. So presenters on youth programmes tend to speak in excited, breathless tones, to give the impression that something dynamic is always going on. Magazines and newspapers also adopt a

particular tone in which they talk to the reader. The tone of such popular newspapers as *The Sun* is conversational, while that of such serious newspapers as *The Times* is formal.

- **The subjects covered.** A popular quiz show screened during the early evening is unlikely to ask in-depth questions about chemistry. However, *University Challenge* or *Mastermind*, screened mid-evening, may well ask questions on the subject.

Media producers would say that they tailor their programmes and publications to the needs of their audience by using these typical reader or viewer positions. Others argue that what the media producers really do is create viewers and readers who live their lives according to what they see on TV and read in magazines.

The 'lads mag' Loaded and The Lady – two publications with sharply contrasting audience profiles

Media Studies audience research

Media producers are not the only ones interested in audience behaviour. Researchers in Media Studies devote much time and energy to finding out who watches, listens to or reads what. They are particularly keen to discover how people of different ages, sex and social class use the media. They use

techniques similar to those used by commercial researchers, and ask such questions as:

- Are some programmes watched more by men than women? If so, why?
- Do children take television dramas aimed at them seriously?
- Which social classes read newspapers, and why?

The importance attached to certain types of programme by different people is also an area of key interest. Men, for example, may view documentaries as being of greater value than soap operas.

How and where do we become an audience?

One area of much interest to Media Studies research is what is called the viewing, listening or reading context, or where the audience comes into contact with media products. The places in which the audience comes into contact with media products change over time, because of developments in media technology and social trends.

Before the introduction of television, most people relied on the radio as a source of information and entertainment. It became a habit in many homes for families to gather together around the 'wireless set'. The tradition was carried on when TV sets became a common feature of most households.

If you draw up a map of most sitting-rooms, you will find that the television set is the central point around which the rest of the furniture is organised. This has implications for the way family life is structured. The television, rather than the other people in the room, becomes the focal point of attention. This, some say, leads to a breakdown in communication within families, as everyone is too busy watching TV to talk to each other. Others argue that television promotes communication as it provides material for family members to talk about.

An interesting area of audience research looks at the issue of who has control over what is watched on the TV – the father, mother or children.

"Today, watching television often means fighting, violence and foul language – and that's just deciding who gets to hold the remote control."
Donna Gephart

The replacement of radio with television led radio producers to look for other listening contexts. A major new listening context was offered by the development of in-car entertainment. Drive-time, or the hours when most people are driving to and from work, has become a peak period for radio consumption. Many radio stations have tailored their broadcast formats to meet the demands of the drive-time audience, providing a mix of music, traffic and weather reports. Another listening context targeted by radio producers is the workplace, with such features as 'office of the day', live coverage of community events and live outside broadcasts.

*Facing page:
Early adverts
placed TV firmly
at the centre of
famly life*

The introduction of the VCR (video cassette recorder) into people's homes led to a revolution in viewing habits. The VCR, which was later superseded by the DVD recorder and hard disk recorders, such as Sky Plus, allowed viewers to:

- **Tape one programme while watching another.** This increased the possible audience for a programme, as people did not have to make a choice between watching one programme or another.
- **Tape programmes while they were out.** This again increased the possible audience for a programme, as people who would have missed it could now record it. Also, viewers were no longer tied to the scheduling of the TV companies.
- **Buy or rent pre-recorded tapes/DVDs and watch them at home.** This could reduce the size of the possible audience for a programme, as viewers had a greater range of options from which to choose.

The launch of the VCR was also expected to have a major impact on cinema. It was widely believed that if people were offered a choice between watching a film at the cinema or in the comfort of their own home, they would opt to stay at home. As a result, it was predicted that cinemas would disappear from our towns and cities. To some extent this did happen, and many old independent picture houses closed because of a fall in customer numbers. The rise of the VCR also led to the development of the made-for-video film – a production that is not shown at cinemas and can be seen only on video. Although it went through a radical change, however, cinema did not disappear. The development of multi-screen complexes attracted a new audience for films. The complexes owed much of their success to the fact that they made going to the cinema into an occasion. Surround-sound, luxury seats, fast food, drinks and special showings all contributed to this. In an interesting twist, video rental shops then began to look more like cinema foyers, with pop-corn and ice-cream on sale.

More recently, audience consumption patterns have been further modified by the arrival of many services that permit audiences to receive media products on demand. Pay-per-view movies from Sky, for example, start at frequent intervals so that audiences can determine the time they wish to start viewing. The convergence of internet technology and the traditional television set allows

Sales of popcorn and icecream have helped cinemas to survive the threat from video

people to download a whole range of archived material, while the advent of the hard disk recorder, sometimes in the form of a computer with its own television tuner, allows audiences in effect to 'pause live television' so that they do not miss any of their favourite programmes. In the near future, these technological developments are likely to further change the way in which people view television, listen to the radio and consume print media.

Broadband technology with its fast download speeds is an important instrument of change in the way that we consume media. Most media producers have a presence on the web. Newspapers, for example, use the internet to create online versions of their titles. Many exploit the technology both to reproduce their newspaper on the web and to provide added facilities. For example, it is easy to include video news reports on a website. Many sites also offer a search facility so that readers can easily locate stories and features in back issues. Online newspapers can provide links to advertisers' sites.

One of the real advantages to advertisers of using the web is that their advertisements can be placed at precisely the point where people are looking for information about the goods or services they provide. Look how when you put any search into Google or Yahoo the results always offer you several sites advertising a product linked to the words in your search.

Computer games have also affected the way people use the media. Many computer games run on television sets. This means that people use their television sets for playing games rather than for watching programmes, which reduces the audience for TV programmes. On the other hand, some people own more than one television set, so a spare can of course be used to watch TV when a computer game is being played, and this increases both the possible audience for TV programmes and the market for television sets. Other games and education systems run on computers with their own monitors, or on hand-held systems, a factor that again reduces the number of people available to watch television. This could, however, offer radio producers a new listening context: computer time.

REVIEW

In this chapter we considered whether the media is a positive or negative influence. We looked at the way in which audiences are increasingly becoming segmented into smaller groups. We explored the ways in which audiences are participating in and influencing media output. We also discussed how information on audiences is gathered and used, and looked at the ways in which technology is influencing how audiences consume media products.

6 Cinema

To watch a film at the cinema is to be part of a piece of trickery. Film is an optical illusion, a play of light onto a screen that the audience reads as a three-dimensional space in which the joys and fears of people's lives are acted out. In 2005, people in the UK made 164 million visits to the cinema, paying nearly £770 million for the privilege of being tricked, such is the popularity of the cinema today. The worldwide figure for cinema admissions is a staggering 9.6 billion.

"Cinema is the most beautiful fraud in the world." **Jean-Luc Godard**

In this case study, we will be examining in detail the cinema as an industry, the making of films and their exhibition both at cinemas and at home, on video/DVD and television.

Sound and vision

Film is able to weave its magic spell over us through a phenomenon called persistence of vision. Most of you will have seen a simple flick book, or even a device like a zoetrope, in which a series of still images is animated to create the illusion of movement. This happens because images remain within your vision after they have actually disappeared, which means that your brain will link a series of still images together to create continuous movement.

A projector is basically a movie camera in which the light is on the inside. A powerful bulb enlarges the 35mm image of the frame to 300,000 times its size on screen.

When we watch a film at the cinema, a strip of celluloid film is pulled through a projector, a machine that consists of a powerful light behind a lens. As each frame passes between the light and the lens, it is projected onto the screen for 1/24th of a second, before the next frame is pulled into the gate and appears on the screen. At the same time, a shutter opens and closes in synchronisation with the frame movement, so we don't see one frame replacing another.

What we are seeing is very like a slide show in which images are shown so quickly that we are deceived into believing we are watching a continuous sequence of events. If you watch early silent movies, you will notice that they flicker (the cinema used to be called the flicks) and the movement of the characters is jerky. This is because they were shot and projected at 16 frames per second (fps), rather than the present-day 24 fps.

Sound first came to the cinema in the 1920s, when films were known at the 'talkies'. Today, sound plays a key role in the enjoyment audiences get from watching film. Film sound usually comes in the form of an

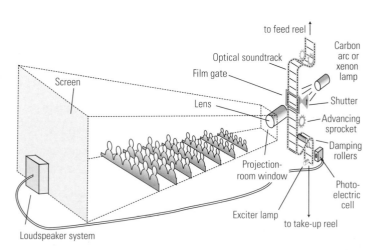

Screen
Lens
Optical soundtrack
Film gate
to feed reel
Carbon arc or xenon lamp
Shutter
Advancing sprocket
Damping rollers
Projection-room window
Photo-electric cell
Exciter lamp
to take-up reel
Loudspeaker system

optical soundtrack, as part of the 35mm print (a positive copy of a film) on which most films are distributed. This track has a light shone through it by a small bulb called an exciter lamp. The beam of light is then picked up and read by a photoelectric cell, which converts light into electrical impulses. These impulses are then fed through an amplifier into the speakers, where they appear as sound.

When the first talkies began, a single loudspeaker behind the screen produced the sound for the audience. The auditorium of a modern cinema contains a number of strategically placed speakers to produce dramatic sound effects, including surround sound, whereby the audience can be made to feel a part of the action of the film. One of the earliest films to exploit the technological possibilities of surround sound was Francis Ford Coppola's *Apocalypse Now*, which was set during the Vietnam War. The director made the film to be projected with quintrophonic sound – three speakers at the front and two behind the audience. This gave the audience the impression that they were not just watching a war movie, but were in the middle of the fighting.

Today audiences expect a quality soundtrack when they visit the cinema. One way in which this is achieved is with digital theatre system (DTS) technology, in which sound is stored on a separate CD-ROM synchronised to the film image. DTS was premiered with Steven Spielberg's *Jurassic Park*.

> "It's a giant leap forward for those of us who create movies and, perhaps more importantly, for everyone who sees them. Digital cinema will increasingly become the standard and will change the way movies are made, seen, and experienced around the world." **George Lucas**

When a film arrives from the distributor for exhibition at the cinema, it comes in reels. On each side of the 35mm print with its optical soundtrack are sprocket holes, which sprockets on the projector use to pull the film through the gate. The film slowly unwinds from a spool above the projector and winds back to one below it. This technology has been around for many years and may seem rather old and cumbersome in a digital age. Film distributors are, however, now using digital technology to beam films direct to cinemas via satellite links. This involves compressing films into encrypted digital signals, which are then decoded and reconstituted into a film shown in the cinema. Besides the advantages of saving on the cost of transporting reels of film around the country, every performance is beamed live by satellite from an original print. This means there is no copy of the film at the cinema to get scratched or damaged every time it is shown.

However, some commentators are seeing this as yet another threat to the future of the cinema. If the latest films can be beamed direct to the cinema, why not beam them direct to the audience at home?

An early 3D cinema screening holds the audience spellbound

Going to the cinema

Going to the cinema has always been an exciting experience. In 1946, before the arrival of television, the British made a total of 1,640 million visits to the cinema. The popularity in the early 1980s of the mass-produced video recorder, together with the chance to rent the latest releases on video, reduced this grand total to 54 million in 1984, less than one visit to the cinema that year for each member of the population.

When TV first arrived, the cinema industry was worried that this new competitor would ruin its business. To try to maintain its lead, the cinema introduced several technical innovations. Some, such as CinemaScope or widescreen, were a success, others, such as 3D and Cinerama, were less successful.

Today cinema has recovered much of its popularity, with audiences almost trebling to nearly 143 million in 2000, which means that on average we all go to the cinema at least twice a year. The apparent threat posed by video and DVD rental outlets and, more recently, satellite movie channels has, in fact, stimulated interest in film-going and led to an increased demand.

The Vue Cinema, Swansea is a typical multiplex

One of the reasons for this increase in cinema audiences in the past decade is the arrival of the multiplex (a cinema complex with numerous screens). The first UK multiplex cinema, based on an American concept, was opened in Milton Keynes, a town that previously did not have a cinema. There are now over 1,700 screens across 185 multiplex sites throughout the UK, including the Warner Village in Birmingham which boasts 30 screens.

A typical multiplex cinema is situated out of town, with good road access. It is close to other amenities, such as shopping facilities and restaurants. It gives the cinema-goer access to around ten screens. Shared projection rooms, box office and kiosks mean that the costs of running so many screens are comparatively small in terms of labour and capital. It also means it is more likely that audiences will find at least one film that they will want to see. Multiplex cinemas have been criticised, however, for appearing to offer audiences a wider choice of films, while in fact reducing what is available. Critics point to the fact that blockbuster releases often occupy several screens in order to pack in audiences, so that a twelve-screen multiplex may actually offer as little as seven or eight films.

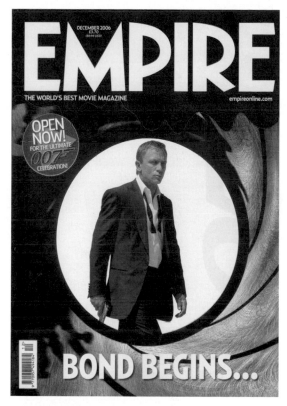

Persuading people to attend regularly is an important ploy in the marketing of cinemas. Of course, their out-of-town location, often at a major road junction, makes it almost essential to have or use a car to get to a multiplex. This has an important bearing on the type of audience that multiplexes attract, as does the fairly high admission prices they charge.

In general, the multiplex is geared to showing mainstream commercial films, usually Hollywood products, which have been well hyped in the media. Occasionally, films that do not have a mass appeal are screened, but these are very much a minority. For example, some multiplexes regularly screen films that have a specific appeal to Asian audiences.

The timing of the release of films is quite important to distribution companies in their efforts to ensure a good financial return on a film. Most films have their premiere in London before going on general release and being shown across the country, usually a week or so later.

Advance publicity for the Bond film Casino Royale, *premiered in London in 2006*

Increased interest in the cinema has also led to a more secure position for what are sometimes called art house, or independent, cinemas. These are cinemas committed to showing films that would not normally be on general release. They may be foreign films, or those made by independent production companies that may not have the mass appeal of Hollywood films. The finances of some independent cinemas are supported by organisations like the British Film Institute (BFI), which helps fund a network of regional film theatres committed to showing films that otherwise might not be commercially viable. There may be one in a town or city near you.

Buying a cinema ticket has undergone some big changes in recent years, largely because of internet technology. Most cinema chains have been quick to see the advantages of selling cinema tickets online as well as over the telephone. A more recent innovation in the sale of tickets has been brought about by Stelios, the man behind the airline Easyjet. EasyCinema works in a similar way to the airline booking system. People who book online well ahead to see films that are shown at less popular times can pick up tickets for as little as 20p. This provides a clear incentive to seek out screenings of films at times when cinemas might expect to have very few customers.

Films and TV on video

Of course, you don't have to go to the cinema to see a film. Films on television have always been popular and people in Britain are especially fond of the video or DVD, either rented or bought. In fact, more than half of UK homes now possess a DVD player. In 2003, the British public rented 88.6 million DVDs and 71.9 million videos. The rental market has declined in the face of competition from cable and satellite, while the retail market has grown – much of this is due to video sales of films targeted at young children, such as Disney productions. There has been a huge amount of growth in online rental over the last two years, and it is expected that by 2009 more than 50% of DVD rentals will be online.

The online DVD rental market has grown significantly in recent years

Films become available as video rentals only after being shown on general release, and perhaps after they have been replayed in one or two independent cinemas. Films available from video rental shops usually have a 'hold-back' period of around six months, during which time the distribution company will not make them available for screening on the satellite channels. This means that the video rental shop has an opportunity to recover its outlay on the film before satellite audiences can watch it. Finally, the rights to a film are bought by one of the terrestrial channels to be shown across the network.

Aspect ratio means the relationship between the width of a screen and its height. An aspect ratio of 4:3 means that the screen looks like this.

High Definition TV offers greatly improved image quality

Films form part of the basic programming of the terrestrial TV channels. When a major film is shown for the first time on one of these channels, it is often accompanied by a similar hype to when it was first released at the cinema. In addition, satellite subscribers can have access to several movie channels, with some channels showing older films as part of the package.

Some people like to create in their own home the viewing conditions that cinema audiences enjoy. Terrestrial television broadcasts many films in NICAM or surround sound, which give stereophonic sound through a compatible TV or through a hi-fi system. Satellite also offers films in surround sound. Viewers must set up five speakers in the viewing area in order to enjoy the full benefits of this system.

Another innovation is the development of widescreen TV. The standard aspect ratio (see above) of a television is 4:3, roughly equivalent to academy ratio, the Hollywood standard before CinemaScope. Films shot for the cinema in widescreen have to be cropped or have part of their image selected for viewing on a standard TV, a technique called 'pan and scan'. Alternatively they can be shown in 'letterbox', with black spaces at the top and bottom of the screen. Widescreen TV, with a ratio of 16:9, allows almost all of the image of a CinemaScope film to fill the screen. After a slow start, widescreen is gaining popularity in the UK, especially as more programmes are being transmitted in this format and the price of the hardware is gradually decreasing. The advent of HDTV (High Definition Television) means increased clarity and detail, making larger screen sizes more comfortable to watch.

Hollywood and the film industry

Whether you watch a film at the cinema or at home, there is a good chance it was produced in the USA. Hollywood is almost the same thing as the film industry, and the majority of films on show at your local cinema are likely to have been made there.

'Bollywood' studios produce more than 900 films every year

There are, of course, other film industries. In India, films are in great demand, not only for the home market, but for export to Asian communities across the world. The Indian film industry, sometimes known as 'Bollywood' (a mixture of the words 'Bombay' and 'Hollywood'), produces more than 900 films a year. In Europe, the French have been active film producers ever since the first public showing of a film by the inventors of the 'cinematograph', the Lumière brothers, in Paris in 1895. Film is seen by many countries as an important part of their cultural identity.

In the UK, many of the films made are financed by the US film industry with an eye for US box-office success. In 2005, 124 films were made in the UK at a total cost of £568.8 million, which means that the average budget for each film was £4.59 million. Much of this figure represents investment from the US. By contrast, the average Hollywood film cost £60 million in the same year. To this should be added £36.2 million of marketing costs by way of prints for distribution and advertising.

The British film industry itself, however, is still capable of producing movies that make a lot of money on both sides of the Atlantic. Made for around £30 million, *Love Actually* took £36 million at the UK box office. It grossed a further $59 million in the USA and $245 million worldwide.

> "Cinema in India is like brushing your teeth in the morning. You can't escape it." **Shahrukh Khan**

Every Hollywood producer dreams of producing a blockbuster – a film that will produce huge box-office receipts, like Peter Jackson's *Lord of the Rings* trilogy. Increasingly, the box-office takings for such a film are only one part of its success story. Spin-offs from a film, including sweets, games, toys and clothing such as T-shirts, are a key ingredient in maximising profits. They also fulfil an important role in the marketing of the film, not only by drawing attention to it, but by holding the audience's interest for longer than success at the box office alone would normally manage to. Films such as *Star Wars* and *Batman* have grossed more from their spin-off earnings than they actually took at the box office. (The 'gross' is the total revenue that a film brings in.) These are sometimes called event movies and are often accompanied by a huge amount of hype across the media before their nationwide release, which is often timed to coincide with school holidays, when families are most likely to go to the cinema.

	All-time top 20 movies at the box office (worldwide)			
	Released	**Film Name**	**Director**	**Total Box Office**
1	1997	*Titanic*	James Cameron	$1,835,300,000
2	2003	*The Lord of the Rings: The Return of the King*	Peter Jackson	$1,129,219,252
3	2006	*Pirates of the Caribbean: Dead Man's Chest*	Gore Verbinski	$1,058,543,455
4	2001	*Harry Potter and the Sorcerer's Stone*	Chris Columbus	$968,657,891
5	1999	*Star Wars: Episode I – The Phantom Menace*	George Lucas	$922,379,000
6	2002	*The Lord of the Rings: The Two Towers*	Peter Jackson	$921,600,000
7	1993	*Jurassic Park*	Steven Spielberg	$919,700,000
8	2005	*Harry Potter and the Goblet of Fire*	Mike Newell	$892,194,397
9	2004	*Shrek 2*	Andrew Adamson	$880,871,036
10	2002	*Harry Potter and the Chamber of Secrets*	Chris Columbus	$866,300,000
11	2003	*Finding Nemo*	Andrew Stanton	$865,000,000
12	2001	*The Lord of the Rings: The Fellowship of the Ring*	Peter Jackson	$860,700,000
13	2005	*Star Wars: Episode III – Revenge of the Sith*	George Lucas	$848,462,555
14	1996	*Independence Day*	Roland Emmerich	$811,200,000
15	2002	*Spider-Man*	Sam Raimi	$806,700,000
16	1977	*Star Wars*	George Lucas	$797,900,000
17	2004	*Harry Potter and the Prisoner of Azkaban*	Alfonso Cuarón	$789,458,727
18	2004	*Spider-Man 2*	Sam Raimi	$783,577,893
19	1994	*The Lion King*	Roger Allers	$783,400,000
20	1982	*E.T. the Extra-Terrestrial*	Steven Spielberg	$756,700,000

How a film is made

The team

Wherever a film is made, the process is likely to be very similar. A key player at all stages of the production is the producer. Before any film is shot, a good deal of planning has to take place: with such vast sums of money at risk, pre-production – as the planning stages are called – is vitally important. The producer's job at this stage is to come up with an idea for the film, get it scripted and raise the money to make the picture. The idea may be the producer's own, or one bought from someone else. Wherever it comes from, a writer will be needed to turn the idea into a screenplay (script).

Directors let the actors know exactly what they want from the scene

Once a producer has come up with or acquired an idea, commissioned a writer to produce a screenplay and found people to put up money for the film, then he or she must hire actors and technicians to work on the film.

The most important member of this team is the director. The director's job is to turn the screenplay into a motion picture. He or she is concerned mostly with the artistic qualities of the film; in other words, the interpretation of the screenplay into a full-length movie. The artistic interpretation on the part of the director is likely to be one of the hallmarks of the film. Many directors give their

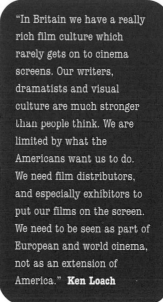

films a personal stamp or signature, which makes it identifiable as their work.

Although a film may be seen as the personal vision of a director, he or she is only the head of a large team of people who are responsible for making the film. As the music plays over the end credits of a film at the cinema or on television, notice the long list of names and jobs that appears. Each person has contributed in some way to making the picture, right down to the important function of providing food on set for the actors and technicians.

> "In Britain we have a really rich film culture which rarely gets on to cinema screens. Our writers, dramatists and visual culture are much stronger than people think. We are limited by what the Americans want us to do. We need film distributors, and especially exhibitors to put our films on the screen. We need to be seen as part of European and world cinema, not as an extension of America." **Ken Loach**

Shooting

Once the producer has got a team together, work can start on the shooting of the film. A schedule has to be drawn up that makes the best use of all available resources, locations, stars of the film and other actors and technicians. Things like stunts, which take a lot of organising, are built into the schedule. Obviously, it makes sense to shoot all the scenes that take place in one location together, regardless of the order in which they appear in the finished film.

The film footage shot each day is called the rushes. These are processed quickly so that the director and other key member of the crew can view them before the next day's shooting.

Film is generally shot on 35 mm film (this figure measures the width of the frame), which is the same size that is used in many still cameras. Formats such as 16 mm and 8 mm are also available. A form of 8 mm film called Super 8 was very popular with amateur film-makers, but has been largely superseded by video. Occasionally film-makers use Super 8 to give a home-made quality to a sequence in a film. Sound is recorded separately. The clapperboard, on which are chalked details of each take (that is, each uninterrupted sequence between edits), is used to ensure that at the editing stage sound and vision will be in perfect 'sync'. This is especially important for dialogue: audiences quickly spot the slightest error in lip sync, when an actor's lips move in different time to the words spoken.

Many films are dubbed into a different language. This means that the original pictures are used, but other actors speak the words translated into a different language. Of course, it is immediately obvious that the lip sync is completely out in this situation, as the movement of the actor's lips does not match the words that are being spoken.

The process in which everything is arranged in front of the camera is called mise-en-scène, as explained in the chapter on media language (see page 21). Each shot at this stage has to be carefully planned to ensure, for example, that continuity will be achieved at the editing stage (see below). Continuity means that all details in a shot will match the details in the next one, even though they may be filmed several weeks apart. An actor who is seen to board a plane in Los Angeles will need to look the same when he or she leaves the plane in New York. If their clothes and hair length are different, for example, an audience will notice the lack of continuity between the two shots.

Editing

"The essence of cinema is editing. It's the combination of what can be extraordinary images of people during emotional moments, or images in a general sense, put together in a kind of alchemy."
Francis Ford Coppola

Once a film has been shot, then the business of editing can begin. Modern techniques of editing film involve the use of computers and video equipment. Film is transferred to video tape and edited electronically, with a computer coding each frame of the original film. Before the digital age traditional skills were used by the film editor. Film was literally cut and stuck together with tape to join scenes. This is called splicing.

An editor's job is to choose which of a series of takes to use. One scene may have been shot a number of different ways. Some of these takes may be unusable for technical reasons, for instance, a problem with lighting or sound. In others, actors may have forgotten or fluffed their lines. (Takes that go wrong and are not used are called out-takes and are very much in demand as DVD extras or the source of such programmes as It'll Be Alright on the Night.) The editor's other main job is to join the chosen shots together into a logical and coherent narrative. In addition, sound used as part of the film has to synchronise perfectly with the movement of an actor's lips on screen.

What's in a name?

There are quite a lot of unusual names given to the jobs in the film industry. Here are some that you are likely to come across most frequently.

Gaffer: chief electrician on the set, takes charge of the lighting

Best boy: the gaffer's assistant (who can, of course, be a girl)

Focus puller: assistant camera operator, whose chief job is to keep the shot in focus when the camera is moving

Key grip: in charge of the grips, or stagehands, who look after the set and the props

Animal wrangler: trains and looks after the animals

It is said that if an editor has done a good job, the audience won't even know it has been done at all. This process of producing films that are seamless is called continuity editing. Audiences are fooled into thinking that there are no edits because the skill of the editor is to match each shot perfectly with the one before and the one after. This ensures perfect continuity within the film. None of the actors does anything illogical. So continuity is an important element in the editing process. If a character is seen to walk in opposite directions when two scenes are edited together, it can be hard for the viewer to make sense of the action.

Film buffs like to find examples of things that go wrong with continuity in films. Have a look at the Internet Movies Database (*www.imdb.com*) and see some of the howlers film fans have noticed in your favourite movie.

Filming a scene from The Lord of the Rings *trilogy*

Some films use long takes, whereas others use edits in quick succession. Next time you watch a film, look carefully at where the edits are placed and how often there are any edits. Then consider what impact this has upon you as you watch the film.

The edited version of a film is called a cut because the film has literally been cut into its final shape. This may not, however, be the cut that you see in the cinema. Different countries have different attitudes to censorship, and this is one reason why the version you see in the cinema in this country may be different from that shown elsewhere in the world. Equally, there is a growing fashion in different cuts, in the same way that there are different mixes of sound recordings. A video release version may even contain scenes not shown in the cinema. A DVD allows a host of extras to be included, such as alternative cuts, documentaries showing the production process and interviews with the stars and director.

Glamorous stars are a powerful force in attracting audiences to the cinema

You may also come across the director's cut of a film, either showing at the cinema or on DVD. Sometimes the version of the film that is released in the cinema is a compromise between the artistic vision of the director and the financial pressures imposed by the production company. Sometimes the cut released in the cinema is considered more likely to appeal to audiences. The director's cut of a film is often released some time later. It is intended to be the director's opportunity to show the version of the film that he or she really wanted. Some people, however, have suggested that the director's cut is often little more than a way of repackaging and selling the same product.

Marketing the film

The star system

In the chapter on institutions, we looked at the importance of stars as a means of helping a producer ensure the success of a media product (pages 56–57). Nowhere is the system more powerful than in the film industry based in Hollywood. The stars are the public face of the film industry; they are the people with whom the audiences are most familiar. As such, their key function is to get people to the cinema. Audiences will go to see a film because of the star.

The film industry has always been clever at promoting itself and its products. Such events as the Oscar ceremonies, and film festivals such as Cannes, held each May in the south of France, attract a vast amount of media attention from across the globe.

What stars do off screen is often as important or even more important than their performance on screen. Gossip is an age-old method of keeping the stars in the public gaze. Stories of stars' private lives, whether true or not, are a way of ensuring constant media coverage and speculation among their fans.

Stars attract fans, who will not only want to watch their films, but are interested in their lives. Stars, therefore, are a powerful force in the marketing of a picture; they are often at the forefront of fashion and lifestyle, introducing the public to new ways of doing things. As trendsetters, stars often become associated with products that they are seen to endorse. Equally, the manufacturers of luxury goods such as cars and clothing are keen to have their products associated with the glamorous lifestyles of the stars. You will often see these products used as props in films. This is known as 'product placement'. It is an effective method of advertising, especially if the film is a huge box-office success.

The more important a star, the more power he or she has. Stars like Clint Eastwood, for example, are able to set up their own companies and direct their own films. This is a far cry from the days of the studio system, where all the major stars were under contract to make a certain number of films to studios such as Warner Bros, MGM and Paramount. Stars who were not co-operative in fitting in with the demands of the studio bosses would find their careers in ruins.

You might like to consider what the appeal of stars is. Stars are generally sexy and glamorous. It has been suggested that their appeal is that they represent the people we would like to be, more perfect versions of ourselves. Stars are often divided into categories. For example, we talk about superstars, those

Hollywood favourites like Brad, Tom and Angelina, who can command huge payment for appearing in a film and whose name is a guarantee of success, or at least so the production company hope.

Reviews

The film industry relies heavily on publicity in the other media, such as radio, television, magazines and newspapers. Reviews are an important source of information about films. They appear in a number of forms, for example on TV programmes where experts or members of the public offer their opinion of a film. Many magazines carry reviews of films released each month at the cinema, as well as video rental and retail releases. Specialist film magazines, such as *Empire* and *Premiere,* try to cover all the feature films that are released.

Newspapers provide similar information, some of it more detailed and considered than others, and radio stations often have slots in programmes in which newly released films are discussed.

The glare of publicity: Scarlett Johannsen (above) and Keira Knightley (below) face the paparazzi

Specialist magazines carry detailed reviews of films released each month, as well as DVD and rental releases

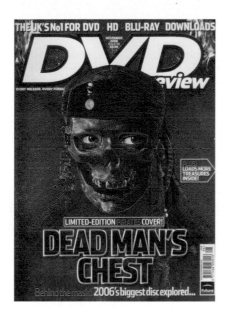

A good film review should be more than just the reviewer's opinion of the film. It should provide potential viewers with information about the film that will allow them to decide whether it is worth seeing or not. For some people, the decision whether or not to see a film at the cinema may rest on the opinion of a reviewer they trust.

REVIEW

As you have seen in this chapter, cinema is an important and complex medium. Like other media products, it is a commodity, produced, in the main, by large and influential institutions. As a commodity, it has to be carefully marketed to ensure that it appeals to as wide an audience as possible. Indeed, as an industry, cinema depends for its survival on this ability to manufacture products that audiences want to consume.

7 Media Technology

This is an exciting time to be involved in studying the media, largely because of the many and far-reaching changes that are currently taking place in media technology. The way in which media is both produced and consumed is changing rapidly. This is having a significant impact upon the way in which both media producers and media theorists think about every aspect of contemporary media.

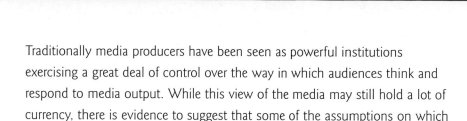

Traditionally media producers have been seen as powerful institutions exercising a great deal of control over the way in which audiences think and respond to media output. While this view of the media may still hold a lot of currency, there is evidence to suggest that some of the assumptions on which this idea is built are being undermined by changes in technology.

Have a look at Chapter 12 on TV news for an example of how this is happening. For many years television news has been regarded as an institution that provides a reliable source of objective and unbiased information. It is very much a one-way communication process in which smartly dressed people sit in smart looking studios telling the audience what is going on in the world. If you tune into a modern day news bulletin, the smart people in the smart studio are still there. What has changed is their desire to involve the audience in the production of the news.

This happens in two ways. Firstly, the interactive nature of modern communications means that newsreaders are able to seek the opinions of viewers through texts, emails, mobile phones and by simply pressing the red button on their remote control. So on any issue the news broadcaster can take a snapshot of public opinion. Secondly, not only can we respond to news, we can be part of it. The use of video cameras available as part of our mobile phone has turned us all into potential news reporters; footage recorded by the public has been used in reporting of events like the 7 July London bombings.

> "The medium is the message." **Marshall McLuhan**

Of course news is not the only area of media production that has been influenced by new technology. As you will see in this chapter, film, radio and print are all undergoing significant changes in the ways in which they are produced and consumed. Some of these changes are also likely to have an important bearing on you as a student of the media, enabling and empowering you to engage with media production technologies in a way that seemed improbable just five years ago.

The way in which we consume the media has always been affected by changes in technology. The invention of photography, the first recording of sound, the introduction of sound into the cinema, or talkies, and the birth of television have all had a major impact on the media and its audiences. One impact of the rapid changes in media technology today is that there are more and more media products available for us to consume. Some people fear that this will result in a society divided in terms of access to media technology and the information and entertainment it provides.

On the other hand, people also argue that changes in technology are leading to the media becoming much more democratic. The power to communicate ideas is no longer controlled by a limited number of powerful people, and is now available to all. Anyone can now get access to the internet and mobile phones and use them as powerful tools to communicate their ideas across the globe.

In this chapter, we look at some of the changes taking place in media technology. We consider how these are likely to affect us not only as individual members of an audience, but also as part of the society in which we live.

Availability and accessibility

> "All of the biggest technological inventions created by man – the airplane, the automobile, the computer – says little about his intelligence, but speaks volumes about his laziness."
> **Mark Kennedy**

One of the key changes is the way in which the media is now able to target individual members of an audience rather than simply broadcasting to a mass market. As individual members of the audience we are likely to be offered a much wider variety of media products to consume, most of them available to us both at home and on the move. These products are much more likely to be designed to meet our individual interests. There is already evidence that the audience for mass media products such as television shows, and mass circulation newspapers and magazines, is in decline. In their place we may end up with a media that is not only targeted at our own specific tastes and needs, but also one that we can call up on demand. No longer will we have to organise our lives around an episode of our favourite soap. Instead we will arrange our consumption of the media around our lives.

This change to patterns of consumption is only just beginning to take shape. A good example of this trend of audiences being able to consume media products on demand is the BBC's decision to make television programmes

Broadband services such as SkyPlus are changing the whole nature of TV as a mass medium

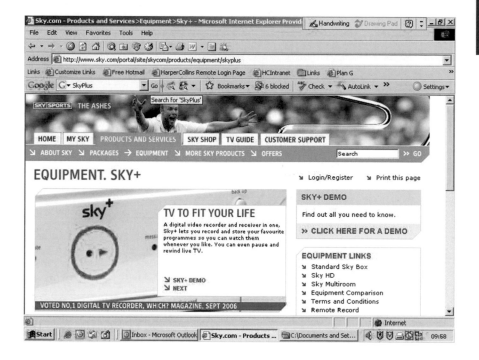

The MyBBCPlayer interface allows viewers to access a wide range of broadcast output

available for download each week through a service called MyBBCPlayer. This allows viewers access to programmes shown in any week on demand as well as access to the extensive BBC archive of television output. Similarly, you can download films on demand from Sky through a broadband connection to your television. The reason that organisations like the BBC and Sky are able to do this is because the speed of internet connections has increased markedly. Today 8 MG download speeds are commonplace, which allows streaming video to provide high quality images on a computer screen. Television on demand is available through services like SkyPlus and Homechoice.

Traditionally, we have always thought of the media as being a mass media. That means that media products are created to be consumed by mass audiences, large groups of people who will access the media through channels such as television, radio and print. This is called broadcast media because it sends its message broadly to most of the population

Comedian Ricky Gervais was among the first to spot the potential of the podcast

and those who are interested will make a point of finding and consuming it. However, narrowcast media is becoming much more important. Narrowcast, as its name suggests, is not intended for the population at large but rather for specific groups of people with a specific interest in a topic or issue. Weblogs and podcasts are good examples of narrowcast media. They rely on a fairly small but dedicated audience of followers to seek them out, consume and respond to them.

Digital radio

"Without (digital), the radio industry signs its death warrant. With it, the industry has a chance to reinvent itself." **Laura Behrens**

Most people who listen to the radio do so by receiving an analogue signal. This signal, which may be AM or FM, can be received on a variety of different radio tuners. These may form part of a hi-fi system, be a small portable radio, perhaps with earphones, or a radio fitted into the dashboard of the car. Some people use their computer to listen to the radio over the internet. There are a number of problems with using an analogue signal to receive radio programmes, one of which is that the signal is easily distorted by atmospheric conditions, such as a thunderstorm, or when it bounces off hills or tall buildings. If you listen to a particular station in your car you may find you have to keep retuning. This is because on the FM waveband a radio station needs several frequencies to cover a large area.

Digital radio signals are able to solve both these problems. They use a binary system, like a computer, which makes them less likely to be distorted than an analogue signal. In addition, they are able to use a single frequency network, which means that all transmitters will use the same frequency for a single programme. Probably the most important advantage of a digital signal is that it allows several programmes to be carried on one block of frequencies, or multiplex. These programmes can be broadcast simultaneously using, in effect, a single frequency.

Currently there are seven multiplexes designated for use in the UK:

- one for national BBC stations
- one for national commercial radio
- five for local radio broadcasting.

Digital radio offers a much clearer sound quality. It also gives the audience a much wider choice. Most people will be able to listen to, on average, 16 national stations and 16 regional or local ones. In addition to most of the existing radio stations, other stations available on digital radio include:

Details of digital radio channels in a listings magazine

- **Planet Rock:** the rock specialist playing uncompromising classic rock from the 60s, 70s and 80s.
- **Core:** fresh hits for the UK. The best of the chart and club anthems.
- **Capital Life:** playing contemporary music for individual, confident, aspirational adults.
- **Oneworld:** the world's first national commercial radio station dedicated to plays, books and comedy.
- **Bloomberg Radio:** 24-hour City, business and personal finance information.
- **ITN:** delivering news, money, sport, weather, travel information and entertainment.

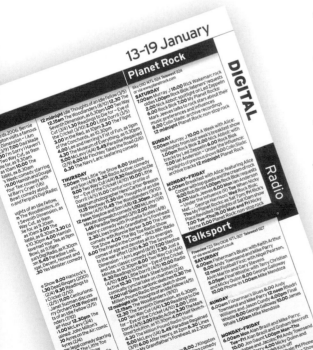

111

The Apple iPod gives users the freedom to listen to music and podcasts wherever and whenever they choose

With a digital signal you can do more than transmit just sound. You can also transmit data. A typical digital receiver is provided with an LCD to allow information to be displayed. For example, a music station will be able to transmit details of the artist, song and album playing over the audio channel. For people listening to radio on the move, information about traffic conditions can be made available, just as it is now.

However, this information, either in the form of voice or text, can be automatically sifted by the receiver, so that only information you need for your particular journey is sent. In effect, the information is customised to the needs of a particular individual rather than being broadcast to a mass audience, many of whom would find the information irrelevant.

More recently, radio has increased its accessibility through the technical innovation of podcasting. Podcasting takes its name from the words iPod and broadcasting. A podcast is basically a radio or video broadcast that can be downloaded from the internet on to a personal listening device like an iPod, although it can also be played on computers. It is then available to the user when he or she is on the move and/or at a convenient time. It also has the advantage that, unlike a portable radio, the sound quality is not subject to deterioration as the listener moves around. What makes podcasting so important, though, is the opportunity that it presents for anyone with access to the internet to create their own radio programme.

Radio has always attracted non-professionals to get involved. Pirate radio, which was very popular in the 1960s, has always existed in isolated pockets in large conurbations, broadcasting illegally, as the name suggests. Much of the attraction of pirate radio broadcasts is the fact that presenters are free to say and do much as they like. The illegality of the operation frees them from the constraints placed on mainstream broadcasters. This can also be true of

Song Name		Time	Artist	Album		Genre	Price	
21 Questions		3:44	50 Cent	⊙	Get Rich Or Die Tryin'	Hip Hop/Rap	$0.99	BUY SONG
Come Close	◀)	4:35	Common	⊙	Electric Circus	Hip Hop/Rap	$0.99	BUY SONG
Ms. Jackson		4:30	OutKast	⊙	Stankonia	Hip Hop/Rap	$0.99	BUY SONG

podcasts, which are able to operate to a large extent outside existing restrictions and regulations. For many people this is an important freedom, not only in this country, but also abroad. People whose freedom of expression has been curbed by repressive governments can use podcasts and other means to express their ideas to the outside world.

Many newspapers are also producing podcasts for their websites, for example, Guardian Unlimited has podcasts of news, sports, science, comedy, etc. Podcasting allows news broadcasters to post interviews for people to download.

During the 1960s and 70s, pirate stations such as Radio Caroline (above) were able to broadcast illegally from ships moored outside UK waters

Print media

Print media, such as newspapers and magazines, have been forced to react to changes in technology in the same way as they had to respond when faced with competition from radio and television. Compared to electronic media, print is much slower at getting its message to the audience. Events that are happening while you sit in class will not be reported in the newspapers until tomorrow morning. Most people will know about them through television or radio news bulletins before they read about these events in a newspaper. As you can see in Chapter 8, print media have met this challenge in a number of ways.

More recently, however, a new challenge has presented itself in the form of online news through the internet. When you connect to the internet, your ISP's homepage usually provides the latest news headlines with a link to the full story behind them. In fact, it is possible to customise many homepages so that you can decide precisely what type of news and information you want. For example, you may decide that you only want to read sports and showbiz news rather than national and international news. This is another example of the way in which the audience is able to shape the precise nature of the media product. Unlike a printed newspaper which tries to cater for all its readers, a website can

Newspapers such as the Mirror, Sun *and* Telegraph *now all provide online as well as printed editions*

be organised to meet the needs of one individual member of the audience.

One way in which print media have risen to the challenge from the internet is to join it. Most newspapers and magazines now have their own websites. Many of them are very similar to the printed or 'hard copy' edition, employing the same headlines and including the same news stories and features. Web-based editions also have a number of advantages over print versions. The main advantage is that they archive, or keep on file, back copies of the paper. Many sites offer a search facility so that a reader looking for an article in a previous edition or seeking information on a topic can use a keyword search. This search will result in a list of articles with hypertext links to take the reader straight to them.

In a similar way, most magazines have set up their own websites, which include features from the current print edition. They do not, however, usually allow access to the entire magazine contents. There is a simple reason for this. Access to most websites is free. If people can read a newspaper or magazine for free, then they will not go out and buy it.

However, the issue is not as simple as this. A high proportion of people still enjoy the convenience of a printed newspaper or magazine. Even though some people have laptop computers with internet access, connecting on a crowded bus or train is a lot more troublesome than simply reading a newspaper. In fact, many print media see their website as a way of promoting the print, or hard copy edition. If people see the newspaper or magazine on the web and enjoy reading the articles, they are likely to go out and buy a copy to read the rest.

Websites are becoming an increasingly important way for magazines to interact with their readers

Another advantage of websites is that they allow people to keep up with news as it happens. Newspaper proprietors are beginning to see the potential of websites as a means of competing with television and radio in their efforts to be first with the news, and many newspaper websites now feature breaking news. (This is news that is just happening and which the news media wants to bring to audiences straight away.) Newspapers would previously have had to wait until the next edition was printed, but they are now able, through their websites, to keep readers completely up to date throughout the day and night. Newspaper websites are also increasingly using video footage to report incidents that are taking place. At last newspapers are finding themselves able to compete with television channels on their own terms.

Newspaper websites can also generate revenue through the use of advertising. This may be in the form of pop-ups which appear on the page you are reading and may often be directly linked to it, as well as links in menus at the side of the page. Such advertising can be targeted quite specifically at the reader. So, for example, if you have opened a page that is telling you about racing, then a

pop-up advertisement offering the services of a bookmaker will be finding a potentially interested person.

It is interesting to see how newspapers have adapted their online editions to use technological innovations like podcasts. *The Sun*'s well-known royal photographer, Arthur Edwards, uses podcasts on the newspaper's online site to offer background information to the photographs he has published in the newspaper.

Other sites ask for your details in order to log you in to their services. By using information about your surfing patterns, such as which pages you visit on their site, they can build up a database of information about you and your interests. This will give them information about your lifestyle and your spending habits. This is ideal information for advertisers who want to target you with information about products you may be interested in.

Websites for the Times online *web video and TV service (top), and for* The Sun's *royal photographer Arthur Edwards*

The idea behind this is called 'push technology'. Rather than having to spend hours searching for information that a person wants, push technology allows a web provider to send specific information based on established patterns obtained from that person's previous surfing habits.

One question that is constantly being asked, given the increased use of internet technology, is how long newspapers and magazines will continue to exist in their present form. Clearly print products of this type have the important advantage that they are portable and designed to be consumed on the move. The decision of many broadsheet newspapers to bring out new compact editions is evidence that newspapers see this as an important selling point. However, as personal communication devices grow in sophistication and become more multi-functional, traditional print publications are increasingly under threat. The music magazine *Smash Hits*, for example, published its last issue in February 2006 and has now become an online edition and radio site.

The music magazine Smash Hits *published its last printed edition in February 2006. It now exists solely in online format*

Television

It is in television that digital technology has had the greatest influence over the way in which we consume the media. Twenty-five years ago, most people had just four terrestrial channels from which to choose their viewing. Two of these, BBC2 and Channel 4, were considered 'minority' channels with a limited appeal. BBC1 and ITV competed for the mass audience, especially in the evening prime-time slots.

The launch of satellite broadcasting in 1989, with four channels, and later Channel 5, meant that the audience was offered a wider range of programming and the opportunity to see films much sooner after their release at the cinema. Although choice had increased, the capacity for broadcasting via analogue technology remained limited. The arrival of digital technology in 1998 allowed an immediate growth to 140 in the number of channels broadcast using satellite technology. Of course, choice comes at a price and many people feel

The Sky News weblog allows digital viewers a quick and easy way to 'look behind' the latest headlines

that a subscription charge of nearly four times the annual television licence fee for an all-inclusive package puts this technology beyond their reach. Some people also argue that there is too much choice, so that it is impossible to keep up with what is available, let alone find time to watch it.

You may also have noticed that digital technology allows viewers further choice, as they can choose variations of a programme within the programme itself. This is particularly useful for sporting events, where several matches or games may be taking place simultaneously and viewers can have a choice of which one they want to watch. This facility is offered by Sky when European football matches are played on the same evening, and is a successful addition to BBC coverage of Wimbledon, where matches take place on different courts at the same time. The BBC also offers a multi-screen news menu that allows viewers with digital receivers to choose from a list of news stories available on demand.

The potential of digital technology is only just beginning to be explored, and choice is only one of the so-called benefits it offers the audience. Until now, audiences have had little or no control over the image on their television screens, other than being able to change channels or switch off. Digital technology allows audiences to control what they see on the screen. For example, most television programmes are shot using a variety of cameras, each with its own angle. The image that appears on our screens is chosen by the director. When we watch a football match, for example, it is the director who decides when we get a close-up of a particular player or whether an action sequence is replayed in slow motion. Digital technology can allow the audience itself to make some of the choices. For example, it is possible to look at a particular incident from the viewpoint of one of the players, wearing a tiny camera called a 'playercam'.

In the same way, we can also select news items that we want to know more about by using the interactive features of Sky News. As you can see, digital technology is capable of handing control over to the audience to play with to suit their own needs and pleasures.

Alongside the development of digital satellite broadcasting, broadband technology is making a considerable impact on the way the media affects our daily lives. Broadband can come in many forms: down a telephone line, through a fibre-optic cable or via a satellite channel. What it does is to bring into your home huge amounts of information at high speed. Current developments in broadband technology mean that moving images can be fed

Japan's Prime Minister Junichiro Koizumi watches a DVD on high-definition TV in Tokyo's electronics district

to your computer screen at such a speed that they can match the quality of those you receive from your terrestrial aerial. Broadband also means that subscribers are permanently connected to the web without having to dial each time they want to use it. At these speeds, it has become possible to watch films as well as having reliable access to music and games.

An important part of all this is that the technology in our homes is beginning to converge. This convergence, as it is called, means that different forms of access to information and entertainment in our homes are beginning to be linked together. At present, most of the electronic equipment in your home tends to be used separately. Some people link their hi-fi to the television and DVD player, while others may use their television to send and receive emails. What new multimedia technology is doing is to bring together broadband technology, internet access and the television in the corner of your lounge. This will not only enable you to receive video on demand rather than visiting your local DVD rental shop or receiving them through the post, but will also open up the way for a rapid expansion of e-commerce or online marketing. This means we will be using our television in a much more interactive way to buy goods and services. We will also be able to send and receive video emails and have a 'virtual' get together of family and friends. What is more, this technology is likely to be available to us both when we are on the move and when we are at home. Without leaving your armchair you will have a world of commerce at your fingertips.

Technology on the move

The ability to communicate away from home has become increasingly important in today's information-rich society. Be it phoning home to find out what is for dinner or making a life-saving emergency phone call, we all see the mobile phone as an indispensable part of our daily lives. However, the mobile phone itself is becoming much more than just a means of getting in touch with people by making a telephone call. Mobile phones are turning into mobile personal communication devices, capable of a range of functions over and above their role as phones for us on the move. Text messaging has become an important part of our daily lives. So has the ability to download music, listen to the radio, take and send photographs as well as record video footage and send and receive emails. Media organisations have not been slow to react to the potential of the mobile phone as a means of communicating their messages to people on the move. The mobile phone is a highly personal means of communication compared with television or newspapers. Messages sent to and received by mobile phones are specific to one individual user. People customise their phones with ring-tones and screensavers that tell other people about themselves and their interests and preoccupations.

The important quality of a mobile phone is that it is a two-way device. Not only is it used to send messages, it is also capable of receiving information from such people as advertisers and television companies. If you would like the latest scores or offers to be sent to your mobile phone, media companies will be keen to do this for you.

One important consequence of this technological advance is that the capacity for making and editing short films is within reach of anyone with the right sort of mobile phone. Suddenly the power to become film-makers and TV producers is within everyone's grasp. Of course, getting work screened is a different matter, even though there are now film festivals dedicated to showing films produced with mobile phone technology. One interesting development is the opportunity presented by the internet to allow people to showcase their work. Sites such as YouTube and Metacafe allow people who have made films to make them available online to anyone who wishes to view them.

The BlackBerry is a wireless handheld device which supports email, mobile phone, text messaging, internet faxing, web browsing and other wireless information services

YouTube provides a platform for people to watch and post videos on the internet. At the time of publication, more than 70 million videos were being watched on the site daily. This includes clips from TV shows, videos about people's hobbies and interests, video diaries, short films, as well as the quirky and unusual. Metacafe has more polished offerings from young filmmakers who haven't been published/commissioned by a mainstream broadcaster. If their material is watched by millions before they are given a TV slot, this gives the TV companies a good clue that they will be popular.

This increased access to production technology also impacts on personal identity. Communities now exist electronically alongside the communities in which we grow up and live. These so-called virtual communities enable people from across the globe to get together online and share knowledge and information. Of course, in a real community, people generally have a good idea of what other people are like, not least because they can see and observe their behaviour. On the web there are no such checks on personal identity and part of the fun of virtual communities is that people can pretend to be someone else. Indeed many people adopt multiple personalities across genders and age groups. An example of a virtual community can be found at secondlife.com, a 3-D virtual world entirely owned and built by its residents. Users create identities for themselves and are able to own land and buy and sell virtual items and services.

The networking sites MySpace, YouTube and Second Life all provide virtual communities in which users can interact online

Interactive technology

Using interactive technology means that we have access to a lot of information, much more than any previous generation. The very fact that it is interactive means, however, that the people who provide this information will in turn have a large amount of information about us. If you use a mobile phone, the phone company knows where you are each time you use it. We are used to being watched by surveillance cameras in shopping malls or on motorways. When we use interactive media, information can be gathered about all the things that we consume, from fast food to fast cars. Knowing what people spend their money on and when they spend it is important information to advertisers. The more they know about people's lifestyles, the better they can target their advertisements.

> "We shape our tools and thereafter our tools shape us." **Marshall McLuhan**

You may have already noticed when you use the internet that advertisements pop up for products that are linked to particular information you are seeking. Some people think that one day we will be constantly targeted in this specific way as vast databases of information about our individual lifestyle are built up. For example, people who like to gamble may be offered odds during a television football match whether a player will score from a penalty. Of course, many people see potential danger here, arguing that our rights to privacy and individual freedoms are being taken away from us. For example, when you use the internet to visit a website, the webserver usually places a 'cookie' on the hard disk of your computer. These cookies are used, often without your knowledge, to store and transmit information about the sites that you visit. It does not take long for a lot of complex and useful information to be built up about a person's interests and tastes.

On the other hand, people also argue that all of this technological change has led to consumers having more control over the media. A popular pastime for some people on the internet is to set up a site so that they can communicate with a potential audience of millions across the globe. These sites often take the form of personal homepages which they use to provide the public with information about themselves, their families and their interests. Some people build sites to celebrate their favourite bands or football teams and share their knowledge and enthusiasm with the world. Some of the best examples of this kind of website can be found on the popular MySpace. The website can be used to share photos, journals and interests, and to build a network of friends. It is also a popular place for bands and their fans to interact.

One impact of new media technology is the way in which it is changing many people's view of the world. For example, people have usually been suspicious of surveillance cameras set up around public spaces, such as shopping malls, to keep an eye on what they are doing. These cameras have been seen as a way of controlling people by watching their every move, like Big Brother in George Orwell's novel *1984*. Now people actually encourage the use of surveillance cameras in the form of webcams on the internet. These can be set up in people's homes to broadcast intimate details of their lives to anyone who chooses to watch.

While we watch Big Brother, *Big Brother watches us...*

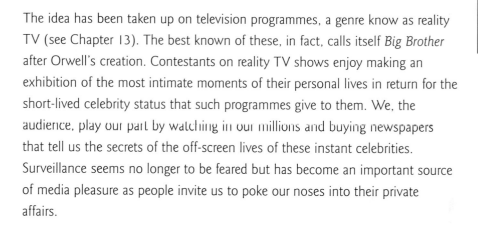

The idea has been taken up on television programmes, a genre know as reality TV (see Chapter 13). The best known of these, in fact, calls itself *Big Brother* after Orwell's creation. Contestants on reality TV shows enjoy making an exhibition of the most intimate moments of their personal lives in return for the short-lived celebrity status that such programmes give to them. We, the audience, play our part by watching in our millions and buying newspapers that tell us the secrets of the off-screen lives of these instant celebrities. Surveillance seems no longer to be feared but has become an important source of media pleasure as people invite us to poke our noses into their private affairs.

Big Brother itself was one of the first programmes to exploit the potential of the internet. Not only was access to the *Big Brother* house available 24 hours a day online, but the audience was also able to use email to make their own direct contribution to the programme. This is a good example of the kind of convergence that is taking place with media technology. Other reality TV shows allow viewers to apply to appear on the show and vote on how issues should be resolved as well.

REVIEW

In this chapter you have explored how technology is changing the ways in which we consume and interact with the media. You have seen how technology allows greater variety in the media, and can often tailor the product to the needs of the individual member of the audience. You have learned how radio, print and television are being changed by technological innovation and how increasingly audiences are able to get access to the media while on the move.

8

Newspapers, Magazines and Comics

On street corners throughout the world, newspaper sellers invite people to read the 'latest'. In airports and stations, kiosks and shops offer eye-catching displays of magazines to entice travellers. In doctors' waiting-rooms, dog-eared piles of old magazines help patients take their minds off their troubles. Newspapers, magazines and comics are some of the most familiar objects on earth.

History

Humans have communicated using writing for thousands of years. However, it was the development of printing in the 15th century that made the written word so powerful. It meant that large numbers of copies of a document could be made, using printing blocks that were covered in ink and repeatedly pressed onto paper. This was revolutionary as it meant that, for the first time, written information could be circulated to a large number of people. Previously, documents had to be copied by hand, which limited their number and therefore people's access to them.

Passengers reading The Daily Herald on a London bus in the 1930s

A revolving printing press introduced by The Times newspaper in the 1840s

At first, though, the development of printing meant little to most people, because they could not read. That is why the earliest newspapers and magazines in the UK were produced for and read by the rich and powerful. The first recognised newspaper or pamphlet to contain information about world events was the *Oxford Gazette*, which was first published in 1665. It was produced to keep the royal court (which had fled to Oxford to escape the plague) informed of events in London. It later became known as the *London Gazette* and is still published today. The first daily newspaper was the *Daily Courant*, published for the first time in 1702. The news it contained was hardly hot off the press, as it carried only stories from papers published on the continent. The history of newspapers really began in the UK in 1785, with the appearance of *The Times*.

The development of newspapers and magazines into items familiar to virtually everyone in the UK was brought about by two main factors: education and distribution. The development of road and especially rail transport meant that newspapers and magazines published in London and other big cities could be distributed throughout the country. But it was only in the 20th century, when most people could read as a result of education reforms, that large audiences for printed material were created.

Newspapers

Thousands of different newspapers are published in the UK each week. They can be separated into groups according to where they are published, and when and how often they are published. Virtually all newspapers fall into the following categories.

Types of newspaper

National daily papers

The national daily papers are the big papers that everyone is familiar with – *The Sun, The Mirror, The Times, The Guardian* and so on. They are published in London each night and are on the newsstands every morning, except Sunday. One traditional method of further dividing up newspapers was between broadsheet and tabloid. Broadsheet newspapers are much larger in size than tabloids and for many people cumbersome and difficult to handle, especially when commuting to work. Broadsheet newspapers were also associated with serious news. Titles such as *The Times* and *The Guardian* prided themselves on the extent and detail of their news coverage, not only in this country but across the globe. They provided serious news about politics, social issues and international affairs. Tabloid newspapers, on the other hand, have always been associated with more trivial and often sensational news coverage. Scare stories and tales of celebrities have always been commonplace on the pages of tabloid newspapers such as *The Sun* and *The Mirror*.

Newspapers about to be loaded onto a train in 1910

In recent years, the format of many broadsheet papers has changed, so that they are now much more like their tabloid cousins. *The Guardian*, for example, adopted the 'Berliner' format in September 2005. Of course, editors of these newspapers would argue that the change in format is a matter of convenience for the reader, rather than a signal that the broadsheets have moved downmarket. It does mean, though, that the traditional distinction by size is no longer valid, so that newspapers are now described as being 'popular' or 'quality'.

The Guardian *newspaper then and now: a typical page in 1945, compared to today's 'Berliner' format*

National Sunday newspapers

As well as national daily newspapers, the UK has a number of national papers that are published only on a Sunday. There are four national Sunday quality papers: the *Sunday Times, Sunday Telegraph, Observer* and the *Independent on Sunday*. The *Sunday Times'* sales are the largest – over 1.3 million every week.

There are seven popular newspapers published nationally every Sunday. They are: *News of the World,* the *Mail on Sunday, The People, Sunday Express, Sunday Mirror, Sunday Sport* and the *Daily Sunday Star*. The *News of the World* sells around 3.5 million copies each week, making it not only the biggest selling Sunday newspaper, but also the UK's best-selling paper overall.

Regional newspapers

Dailies: In addition to the national newspapers produced in London, the UK has a strong regional press. Nearly 90 daily newspapers are published in cities and towns throughout the country. Regional papers tend to be grouped according to what time of day they are published (either in the morning or in the evening), rather than according to whether they are popular or quality. There are only a few morning regional newspapers. They include the *Daily*

Record, which is published in Glasgow and is the UK's biggest selling regional daily newspaper, with sales of over 400,000 copies a day. Most regional daily papers are evening papers. The London *Evening Standard*, for example, is the second largest regional daily with around 325,000 copies bought every day.

Regional morning papers were once popular, but went into decline, largely as a result of competition from national morning papers. In 1999, *Metro*, a free morning newspaper for commuters, was launched. It is distributed in London, Manchester, Birmingham, Leeds, Sheffield, Newcastle, Leicester, Derby, Nottingham, Bristol, Bath, Glasgow and Edinburgh. Every weekday morning over a million copies are distributed across the UK, making it the world's largest free newspaper. According to the Newspaper Society, 84% of all adults (40 million people) regularly read a regional or a local newspaper — far more than those who read a national title.

Weeklies: Most regional papers are published only once a week. These publications can also be separated into two groups, according to whether they are paid for by the reader or given away free. The idea of giving papers away free to readers and making money only from the adverts that they contain became popular in the 1970s. However, economic recessions that led businesses to reduce their advertising budgets forced many free newspapers to close.

Sundays: There are also a number of regional papers that are published only on a Sunday. These include the *Sunday Life,* which is published in Belfast, and the *Sunday Sun*, published in Newcastle.

Specialist newspapers

As well as regional and national papers, there are newspapers that cover specific areas of interest. The *International Herald Tribune* is a daily paper that covers world news. The *Racing Post* is a national

Right: More people regularly read a local than a national newspaper

daily paper that covers events in the world of racing. The *Morning Star* is a daily left-wing political paper that is published nationally. The *New Musical Express* publishes the latest news from the music world, along with reviews and features each week. The *Angling Times* is one of many weekly newspapers that cater for leisure interests.

What's in a newspaper?

The process of putting any paper together is basically the same, although there are thousands of newspapers, each one of them different. Most newspapers have several distinct departments:

*   Editorial, which is responsible for the words written by reporters and the pictures taken by photographers
*   Advertising
*   Production
*   Sales.

Who does what?

The advertising department

Like all media organisations, newspapers have to make money if they are to survive. They get their money from two sources:

*   **Cover price** The price of the paper, which is paid by the reader when they buy it.
*   **Advertising fees** These are paid to the publishers of the paper by the businesses that buy space to promote their products.

The amount of money that a paper makes from its cover price and advertising depends on its circulation, or the number of copies that it sells each day or week. If a lot of papers are sold, as is the case for national dailies, then a large part of the publisher's income comes from the cover price. If fewer papers are sold – for instance, in the case of local weeklies – most of the money comes from advertising. The general rule is that the smaller a paper's sales, the larger the percentage of adverts in it. Free papers that are delivered through every door in a set circulation area make all their money from advertising.

The advertising sales department, under the control of the advertising manager, has the task of selling advertising space to businesses. The advertising manager has a team of sales representatives, who contact businesses either by visiting them or phoning them, the latter known as telesales. Advertisers can pay for their adverts to be put in a specific place in the paper, such as the front or back, or can simply leave the position of the advert up to the newspaper, which is known as 'run-of-paper'.

The types of adverts found in newspapers include:

- **Display adverts** or adverts for products, with photographs and graphics, placed by businesses.
- **Classified adverts**. These are small adverts in columns, usually placed by individuals. They cover such areas as second-hand goods, cars and births, marriages and deaths.
- **Advertorials**. These are advertising features about products, which are written like news stories and are usually accompanied by pictures.

Press advertising is covered in more detail in Chapter 10. However, at this point it is important to realise the crucial role that advertising plays in newspapers. Without money from adverts, most papers would go out of business. (In fact for decades, the front page of *The Times* consisted of nothing but advertisements.) Because of this, great importance is given to advertising by publishers. Adverts are usually placed on a page first and the stories produced around them. This means that the way a newspaper looks depends to a large degree on the adverts that are in it. They make up what is called the 'page scheme', which the editorial department has to work around. Page schemes are plans of news pages that have been drawn up by the advertising department. They show where the adverts that have been sold are placed on the page.

'The best newspapermen I know are those most thrilled by the daily pump of city-room excitements; they long madly for a good murder; they pray that assassinations, wars, catastrophes break on their editions.' **Pete Hamill**

The editorial department

The editorial department produces the 'news' in newspapers – in other words, the stories and photographs that appear around the adverts. The editorial department is usually made up of:

A modern
newspaper editor
at work

A sub-editor chooses
images to illustrate the
paper's lead story

A 1930s newspaper
compositor setting
type by hand

- **The editor**, who is in charge of the whole department. Editors make sure everything runs to plan and have the final say on what appears in the paper. They work closely with the advertising manager to make sure that the paper makes as much money as possible.

- **The chief sub-editor** is a senior journalist with design and layout skills. Chief sub-editors receive page schemes from the advertising department and decide which stories will go on each page. They distribute the page schemes and stories to sub-editors.

- **Sub-editors** are journalists who place stories and photographs on page schemes. They do this on computer screens. Before placing a story and writing a headline for it, they must first check that it is accurate, does not break the laws of libel and is spelt correctly. They do all this under the guidance of the chief sub-editor.

- **The news editor** is a senior journalist who is in charge of a team of reporters. News editors look at all the stories coming in and decide which ones to follow up. They give the stories that they are interested in to reporters and tell the photographic department what pictures will be needed. They also check stories written by reporters before they are sent to the chief sub-editor.

- **Reporters** are senior and junior journalists who research and write stories. Reporters may cover all kinds of stories, or they may be specialists concerned with a specific area of the news, such as sport or crime.
- **Photographers** take and develop the pictures needed for each edition of the newspaper. They are usually controlled by a chief photographer and report to the picture editor, who oversees the photographic needs of the newspaper.
- **Designers** are artists who produce graphics for editorial features and advertisements.

The production department

The production department is responsible for putting the paper together in its final form, as well as for having it printed. The production editor oversees the printing of the paper, working with a team of plate-makers and printers. Printing is the most expensive area of newspaper production: the cost of printing presses runs into million of pounds.

Until the 1960s, newspapers were typeset on machines like this Monotype hot-metal caster

Over the last 30 years, developments in printing technology have revolutionised the production of newspapers.

Hot-metal printing: Until the 1960s, papers were printed using movable metal type, which was built up into pages. The ink was placed onto the type and newsprint was then run over the top of the plates. This form of printing was known as 'hot-metal', as the metal type could be melted down and remoulded to make different letters, words and symbols.

Photo-typesetting: With the invention of photo-typesetting, stories (or 'copy') were typed on computers and then printed onto a special type of photographic paper called bromide paper. This paper was then cut to size and pasted onto page plans, which were photographed. Printing plates were made from the photographs.

Offset litho printing: This was the invention that changed the face of UK newspapers. It involves using photographic negatives of bromide pages to make printing plates with raised images. The plates are placed on printing drums and rotated so that they come into contact with ink rollers. The drums then impress an image onto rubber sheets. Newsprint is pressed onto the rubber sheets and the pages are printed.

The sales department

Once a newspaper has been printed, it has to get to the readers. This is the responsibility of the sales department. Under the sales manager, the department tries to maximise sales of the paper through as many outlets as possible. Outlets include:

*   Newsagents and other shops
*   Paper sellers on the street
*   Home deliveries.

Sales representatives try to persuade shops to take more copies of the paper. They also contact individuals at home to encourage them to have the paper delivered. Special offers are often used to tempt readers to order regular copies of a newspaper.

*A Victorian
newspaper vendor
on the streets of
London*

Distribution

Newspapers are distributed using all forms of transport. National newspapers use rail and air links to send out their publications. Local paper delivery vans are a familiar sight in most towns, as they take the latest edition to the shops. Paper-sellers go to a distribution point to pick up bundles of papers before setting off for their carefully chosen spots throughout towns and cities. Many students are part of a newspaper distribution network, working to deliver papers for a newsagent.

As you can see, the production and distribution of newspapers is a costly and time-consuming business. It also seems a rather dated process in a society that is becoming increasingly dependent on digital technology. To this end, most newspapers now have online editions that can be accessed via the internet and also include features that are not available in the print, or hard copy, editions that people buy at the newsagent. Of course, these online editions also have one major disadvantage, that they are not easy to carry around and read on the way to work or school. However, as technology finds new ways for media producers to communicate with their audiences, it is not beyond the bounds of probability that ways will be found of making newspapers that no longer require paper available in a format that is to some extent portable. In the meantime, let us look at some of the features of online editions of popular titles.

Home page of the Guardian Unlimited website

Online editions of newspapers are usually available free of charge via the web, so anyone with access to an internet-enabled computer can read them. The web-based version is usually similar to the print edition in terms of its content and to some extent its format. However, some online editions, for example, *The Sun* Online, do not provide all of the detailed coverage to be found in the print edition. In fact, *The Sun* Online is actually used to promote the print edition by offering just the 'intro' to some of its major stories and inviting surfers to buy a copy of the paper to get the rest. *The Guardian* offers both an online edition, Guardian Unlimited, and a subscription service whereby the actual print version of the paper can be downloaded via the web. This means that people receive via the web the full edition of the newspaper which they can either read on screen or print out. This option has a clear appeal to people away from home or working overseas. Some hotels abroad offer print copies of British newspapers that have been downloaded in this way.

Online editions have some interesting advantages over their print cousins. The most obvious one is that they can be updated far more quickly with breaking news. News that happens one day will not appear in a national newspaper's print edition until the following morning. It is, of course, a simple matter to include a new story in an online edition as it happens, in the same way as a television or radio bulletin. Similarly online editions have the capability of using both sound and moving images for their stories, while the print editions are limited to still images and the printed word. Of course, both of these features of an online edition may put it into conflict with the print edition, not least because it offers a potentially superior, more up-to-date product. Until online editions start charging surfers for access or generate sufficient advertising volume to cover their production costs and make a profit, developments in these areas are likely to be very limited. A newspaper would be very foolish to put itself out of business.

Online editions of newspapers also provide access to their archives, or back copies of the newspaper. These archives are usually searchable, which means that a keyword put into the search engine will find all relevant stories. This is a particularly useful tool for students of the media who may wish to locate information or details of a news story for a topic they are researching. If you want to use this facility, the newspaper may require you to register with them by providing your email address. Of course, this information is itself useful to the publishers, as it allows them to market information to you about their newspaper and related goods and services.

From story to page

Newspaper stories, like all media products, are the result of a production process that involves a team of workers. To reach the printed page, a story goes through the following stages.

Choosing the story

'News' does not just happen; it is created. Someone has to decide that it is news before it is printed or broadcast. The people who decide this are journalists. In the case of newspapers, it is usually the news editor who judges what the news is. They sift through the stories that come in and decide

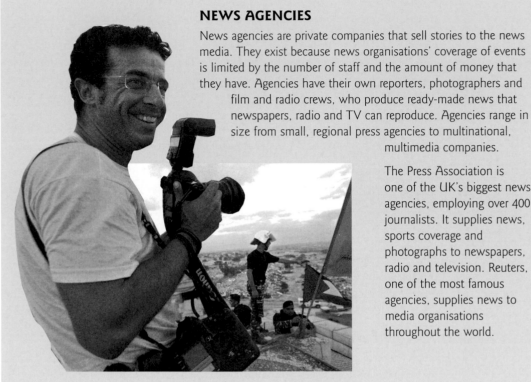

NEWS AGENCIES

News agencies are private companies that sell stories to the news media. They exist because news organisations' coverage of events is limited by the number of staff and the amount of money that they have. Agencies have their own reporters, photographers and film and radio crews, who produce ready-made news that newspapers, radio and TV can reproduce. Agencies range in size from small, regional press agencies to multinational, multimedia companies.

The Press Association is one of the UK's biggest news agencies, employing over 400 journalists. It supplies news, sports coverage and photographs to newspapers, radio and television. Reuters, one of the most famous agencies, supplies news to media organisations throughout the world.

Associated Press photographer Emilio Morenatti working in Gaza in September 2005

whether to follow them up or not (for a list of sources of stories, see Chapter 12). There is a difference between the stories that are reported to a newspaper, and the stories that a newspaper reports.

Not all the information that arrives on a news editor's desk ends up as news in a paper. The news editor decides whether the material that comes to their attention will become news by being turned into a story, or remain unreported information. In this way, news editors influence what the audience thinks of as news. By sorting information and deciding what to follow up, they set a news agenda, which is drawn up on the basis of the news editor's personal decisions, not on the basis of information that they receive. This is why the news is something that is created, rather than simply reported.

News values

Several factors influence whether a story will be selected for coverage. These are often called 'news values' and include:

- **Where the event occurred.** If an event happened within the area covered by the newspaper, it will be more interesting to readers than an event that took place outside it.
- **When an event occurred.** An event that has just happened is more newsworthy than one that happened a week ago. This is simply because people are more likely to know about something the longer ago it happened.
- **Who is involved in the story.** A story is more likely to be reported if the person involved is famous or well known in the newspaper's circulation area.
- **News sense.** This is a word used by journalists to describe a gut feeling about what makes a good story that will interest readers. It is often talked about as if it were a kind of magic power. However, it is really a professional way of looking at information, which is built up through the experience of working in a news environment.

Getting the information

If a news editor thinks that a story is interesting enough, they give it to a reporter. It is the reporter's job to gather all the information they think is necessary to write the story. The news editor briefs the reporter on what the story is about and supplies any information that the newspaper has about it. This may be addresses and telephone numbers, a press release, a report from the emergency services, or copy from a news agency. The reporter then begins to add to this information by interviewing people face-to-face or on the telephone, visiting the site of the event and gathering information from organisations, libraries or other newspapers.

Writing the story

Once a reporter has enough information to write the story, they sit down at a computer and key in the words that make up the copy. This is done using a set of professional codes, or ways of writing that have been learnt from other

TYPES OF STORY

Journalists separate stories into types, depending on their length or the position they are intended to take on a page. Some story types are:

SPLASH – the main story on the front page of a newspaper

PAGE LEAD – the main story on a newspaper page. It is usually the longest story on the page and has the biggest headline

SUPPORT – usually the second largest story on a newspaper page, 'supporting' the main story

SHORTS – stories that are usually between three and eight paragraphs in length

FILLS – stories of no more than one or two paragraphs, which are used to fill gaps on a page

NIB – or news in brief. Nibs are one- or two-paragraph stories that give only basic facts. Nibs are often arranged in lists with small headlines on the front page of a newspaper. They usually refer to stories carried inside the paper and give the page number on which the full story appears, so that readers can find it.

NAG – or news at a glance. These are short review summaries that give the main points of a story.

journalists (see Chapter 2, pages 18–19, for an explanation of codes). In writing the story, they select what information will be included and what will be left out, and decide the order in which the information will appear.

Most news stories are written in the following format:

- **Intro:** This is the first paragraph of the story; it is also the most important one. Research into how people read newspapers shows that most people read the headlines first and, if they find them interesting, will then read the first paragraph of the story. If the first paragraph is not interesting, most readers will not continue with the story. After reading the intro, readers should be able to tell what the story is about. The intro paragraph acts as a 'hook' to drag readers into the story.

- **Elaboration:** The next few paragraphs tell readers more about the story outlined in the intro. They tell readers what happened, when, where and to whom it happened. The elaboration should also say how it happened and, if possible, why. In all news stories, the more important the information is, the closer it is placed to the beginning of the story.

- **Quotes:** Virtually all news stories contain comments from those involved. These are called quotes, and are meant to be word-for-word records of what the person said. They usually come after the story has been elaborated and are important in presenting a balanced view of a story.

- **Projection:** Many, though not all, news stories tell the reader what might happen next in relation to the event or people in the report. This may take the form of a police officer saying what they will be doing in an enquiry, or an MP outlining what action they will be taking over a particular issue. This sort of information is generally used to end stories.

introduction

projection

Tea, but no milk, please:
How to beat heart disease

quote

By Jane Kirby

Tea drinkers have been told to give milk a miss if they want to help their hearts.

Studies show that drinking tea can help protect against cardiovascular disease. But now researchers believe that adding milk counteracts any beneficial effects. When black tea is

drunk on its own, cardiovascular function improves.

The research, published in the *European Heart Journal*, involved studying 16 healthy post-menopausal women. They were given either 500ml of black tea, black tea with 10 per cent skimmed milk or boiled water as a control.

They drank it on three separate occasions but re-

frained from drinking tea for four weeks both before and after the study.

All the women were given a croissant as a standardised breakfast while they drank the tea.

In a healthy artery, blood vessels are able to relax if the blood flow increases. This is called flow-mediated dilation (FMD).

The researchers from the

Charite Hospital Universitatsmedizin Berlin in Germany, measured FMD levels in the forearm using ultrasound. They did this before tea was drunk and at intervals afterwards.

The study said: "Black tea significantly improved FMD in humans compared with water, whereas addition of milk completely blunted the effects of tea."

The researchers believe that proteins in milk, called caseins, could be to blame for the negative effect.

elaboration

The structure of a news story

An important element a journalist must keep in mind when writing a story is that of balance. Journalists must try to give equal weight to the point of view of those involved in the story in order to avoid bias. In theory, if a story is critical to a particular person or organisation, that person or organisation should be offered the chance to respond to this criticism. In practice, however, balance is a controversial issue, as many people believe they have been unfairly treated in the way they are portrayed. Journalists may find it difficult to always equally represent the views of all those involved in stories. Some people, however, accuse journalists of misrepresenting people in order to 'spice up' stories. The issue of balance is important in debates about how different groups in society are represented. As was discussed in Chapter 3, many groups feel that the media is biased against them. Many left-wing councils have complained that stories written about them by journalists who work for right-wing newspapers are biased and without balance. The Press Complaints Commission, discussed in Chapter 4, was set up to deal with complaints about unfair treatment in news stories, amongst other things.

The deadline is the time by which the reporter has to have a story ready. The reporter must make sure that the copy appears on the news editor's screen in time for it to be checked, before being sent to a sub-editor. The news editor reads through the story to make sure that it makes sense and that the reporter has followed up all the possible avenues of information. If they are not satisfied, they will send it back to the reporter with suggestions as to how it could be improved – for example, by interviewing another person.

Getting the picture

Every news story is considered not only in terms of words but also in terms of the photographs or graphics that could accompany it. The news editor looks at each story and decides if there is a photograph that could go with it. If they think that there is, they discuss with the picture editor or chief photographer what sort of picture would be suitable. It may show an event happening, for

instance, a demonstration or a meeting, or it may show a person involved in the news. Once it has been decided what sort of picture is wanted, the task is given to a photographer to go out and take it. The photographer has a deadline for the photograph and has to make sure it is developed in time to be used in the newspaper.

As well as using photographs, the news editor may decide that a story could be illustrated with graphics in the form of illustrations, tables or decoration. In this case, they talk to the design department and a graphic designer is briefed to come up with the necessary graphics.

Sub-editing the story

When the copy and photographs are ready they are sent to a sub-editor. Sub-editors are given page schemes by the chief sub-editor. They are also given a list of stories and photographs to fit onto the page schemes. Their job is to display the stories and photographs to the best effect in the space surrounding the adverts. Their job involves:

- **Making sure stories do not break the law by libelling people:** Libel is a law that defends people's right not to have things said about them in print that are not true and which damage their reputation. If a newspaper

prints a story that libels someone, the victim can take the newspaper to court and demand cash in compensation.

- **Correct spelling and grammar:** Even trained reporters make mistakes.
- **Writing headlines:** Headlines are 'doors' through which readers get into stories. They have to be interesting and inviting, or the reader may pass the story by. This is especially true on the front page, as it is often the main headline that persuades a reader to buy the paper.
- **Placing photographs to best effect:** Photographs are 'windows' through which readers see what is going on in a story. If the photograph is used badly, it will be ignored and fail to attract the reader to the story. This is especially true on the front page. The picture that is used on the front page of a newspaper has to be good to encourage readers to buy the paper.
- **Writing captions:** These need to be written for photographs to tell the reader what they show.
- **Making sure the story fits** into the space set aside for it on the page, usually by cutting words from it. Once a sub-editor has laid out the page, it goes to the chief sub-editor on the computer network to be checked. If it is approved, the page is then sent to be printed.

Newspaper identities

All newspapers have their own identities, which are expressed through:

- Design and layout
- Content
- Language.

Design and layout

Although nowadays many of the quality newspapers share the same tabloid shape as the popular titles, there is a marked difference in their front pages. Popular titles tend to go for 'loud' front pages which seem to shout out for the attention of the reader. Typically they will use a large point size for their headlines, which are often limited to just a few words. If an editor is able to get hold of one, a large dramatic photograph is used to grab the attention of the reader. In consequence, in a popular title there is very limited amount of space for the actual front page story, which is often continued on an inside page.

Quality newspapers, on the other hand, tend to have rather more subdued front pages. Headlines, although larger than the rest of the type on the page, tend to be smaller than those in the popular press. They also tend to contain more words and give a greater indication of what the main story is about. Quality newspapers are also keen to use an illustration which will attract the attention of the would-be reader, although this generally takes up rather less of the front page than in the popular titles.

All newspapers, both quality and popular, are eager to attract readers by splashing details of any free offers, such as DVDs, books or holidays, prominently on their front page, usually employing bright colours to do so.

The contrasting identities of these four national newspapers are reflected in their branding, and in their choice and treatment of front-cover stories

The inside pages of both popular and quality newspapers have obvious similarities with the front pages. Popular titles use large headlines and big illustrations, and the quality newspapers tend to be rather more subdued in their reporting of events.

Content

Newspapers also develop their own identities through the type of story they print. Popular papers, especially *The Sun,* the *Star, The Mirror, News of the World* and the *People,* generally carry stories concerned with crime, sex, gossip and scandal. This has led to them being called the 'gutter press'. They have been condemned by some for lowering moral standards by publishing stories regarded as being in bad taste. Editors of popular newspapers, however, argue that they aim to entertain their readers as much as to inform them. They also say that the fact that their papers have the highest circulations shows that their readers are interested in the subjects they cover. Of course, not all popular papers are like this. What are known as the mid-market papers, such as the *Daily Express* and *Daily Mail,* generally take a less sensational approach and carry more 'serious' news.

Quality newspapers see their job as that of informing their readers about what is going on in the world. Their stories tend to deal with political, economic and international news. It is unusual for a quality paper to lead on a sex scandal, unless it affects politicians or other people in positions of authority.

Language

A major part of a newspaper's identity is the language that is used in stories. The words used play an important role in the way the paper addresses its readers. In Chapters 2 and 5, it was shown that different media products use different tones of voice to communicate with their users. Popular newspapers use short, simple words. They tend to use slang, as some people do in conversation, for example, 'cops' instead of police, and 'squaddies' instead of soldiers. They often refer to famous people by nicknames, like 'Posh' and 'Becks'. They also use puns and wordplay to make headlines entertaining. Popular newspapers have been attacked for using sexist and racist language to describe minority groups and foreigners.

Quality papers tend to use more formal language. Stories often contain longer words and sentences than are used in popular papers. Headlines are written 'straight', in that they rarely use humour or wordplay. People in stories are usually given their proper titles, such as Mr Blair, Mrs Gupta or Ms Anderson.

Magazines

The word 'magazine' comes from the French 'magasin', which means 'shop' or 'storehouse'. This is an appropriate name, as magazines tend to be storehouses of knowledge and information about a particular subject or area of interest. The first magazine to be published using the word in its title was the *Gentleman's Magazine* of London, which was first published in 1731.

Magazines are very different from newspapers. They are generally thicker, printed in colour on glossy paper, and are published less frequently. One major difference between newspapers and magazines is their content. As magazines are published less often, they cannot keep readers informed of day-to-day happenings, as newspapers do. Therefore, magazines tend to focus on feature material, in the form of interviews with 'newsworthy' people, or investigations of particular subjects.

Magazine publishing is one of the most lively areas of media production. There are over 3,000 titles published, generating £1.6 billion from sales to customers. Approximately 350 new titles are launched each year, of which half become established.

So many magazines

Over 7,500 magazines are presently published in the UK. They range from the *Radio Times* to *Dog World*. Magazines are generally divided into two groups:

- **Business and professional titles** These are specialist publications aimed at people in specific areas of business and industry. Such magazines make up the majority of those published in the UK: around 5,000 titles fall into this category.

There is a magazine for virtually every subject you can think of

- **Consumer** These are magazines aimed at the general public, or specific segments of it. They include the publications that most people think of when the word 'magazine' is mentioned, for instance, *Just Seventeen, Cosmopolitan, The Face, More, FHM, TV Times*.

Front covers of style magazine The Face, Marie Claire *and the listings magazine* Time Out

There are so many magazines because they are relatively cheap to produce in comparison with newspapers. This means that there is less risk involved in setting one up. As most magazines do not have their own printing presses, all they need is staff, computer equipment and enough start-up cash to pay a printer. Desk-top publishing (DTP) packages which allow professional-looking pages to be produced on personal computers have revolutionised magazine publishing. Working from a rented office, a small team can have a magazine in the newsagent's within months of the initial idea to set it up.

In Chapter 5, audience segmentation, or the splitting of audiences with particular interests from wider audiences, was discussed (see pages 71–72). The magazine market has seen a large degree of audience segmentation. The low cost of publishing means that a very small readership with special interests can be catered for at a profit. So a publisher might look at existing fishing magazines, decide that they are too general and that money could be made by launching a magazine solely for those interested in fly-fishing.

'Far more thought and care go into the composition of any prominent ad in a newspaper or magazine than go into the writing of their features and editorials.' Marshall McLuhan

However, not all magazines are published to make a profit. Fanzines are magazines with a small circulation that are produced by fans about their particular area of interest, for example, a band or a football team. Fanzines are published on very low budgets, often using basic resources. They tend not to make a profit and are produced out of love for the subject they cover. Increasingly, publishers of fanzines are using the internet as a cheap and easily accessible alternative to print (see Chapter 7, pages 120–124).

Making money

Like newspapers, magazines can make money from their cover price (which the reader pays to buy a copy), from advertising or from a combination of both. Most business magazines are sent free to readers and make all their money from advertising. Consumer magazines generally charge for copies. However, advertising is still their major source of revenue.

Magazine advertising departments work in a similar way to those of newspapers. They sell adverts on the basis of how much space they take up on a page, and which page the advert is on. Most quote a price for a full-page advert in their magazine and, for a smaller advert, work out a percentage based on that price. The more copies a magazine sells, the more it can charge an advertiser, as it can say that more people will see the advert. In 2006, taking out a full-page colour advert in the *Radio Times*, which had a circulation of just over a million copies weekly, cost £39,000. In comparison, a full-page colour advert in *Top Gear* magazine, with a circulation of 175,218, cost £10,752.

One way in which magazines create income that they can rely on is through the subscription system. This is where a reader pays for a set number of copies of the magazine in advance, usually at a price lower than they would pay in the shop. The magazine is then sent to the reader by post. The advantage for the magazine is that it receives a lump sum of money that it can invest in its operation.

A major factor affecting how much money magazines make is the cost of the paper. A steep rise in paper costs can force a magazine to increase its cover price or even to close down.

Setting up a magazine

More and more magazines are being launched. Unfortunately for their publishers, many sink. To make sure that a magazine has a chance of success, potential publishers have to take many factors into consideration.

Identifying a market

A publisher must be sure that there are people who will buy their magazine. It is no use producing a magazine for worm racers if there are only three in the country. Publishers must also be sure that there is enough to write about and photograph on a specific subject to fill a regular magazine. The number of worm racing facts and action shots may be somewhat limited.

*Showbiz weddings and
Big Brother 'exclusives' are
favourite front-cover leads
for celebrity gossip
magazines such as* Heat
and OK!

Assessing the competition

Before launching a new magazine, a survey of the market must be done to see
what magazines are already published in the same subject area. If there are
already a lot of them, it may be difficult to justify launching a new one, as
readers have only so much money to spend. The publisher may decide to go

ahead with the magazine only if they are convinced that it will be better than others already being published and will lure readers away from them. When a particular subject area is seen to be completely covered by magazines, it is known as 'market saturation'. It could be argued that men's lifestyle and computer magazines have reached market saturation point.

Most new magazines are produced because their publishers believe that they have spotted a gap in the market, or an area that is not catered for by existing magazines and that could generate a profitable readership. Look at the number of magazines on the market that cater for the public's appetite for news and gossip about celebrities. Probably the best known is *Hello!* magazine, which specialises in stories about celebrities and features photographs of their homes and families. Launched in 1988, *Hello!* magazine is distributed in 65 countries. It has a UK circulation of 345,000 per issue. Its main rival is *OK* magazine with a circulation of 495,000. *Heat* magazine appeals to a younger audience by publishing stories and photographs of celebrities at events such as parties, clubs and film premieres. It sells 570,000 copies per month.

Attracting advertisers

As most magazines depend on advertising to survive, a publisher has to be certain that some businesses will want to buy space in the new publication. The publisher will have to convince businesses that enough people will read the magazine to make it worth paying for an advert. To do this, they will outline to potential advertisers the readership that they have identified.

Securing finance

The publisher will need cash to set the magazine up. They will have to buy or rent offices and equipment, employ staff and pay for printing. The money may come from a bank loan or from investment by other businesses in the project.

Organising distribution

For a magazine to make money, people have to be able to buy it. Most magazines are sold in newsagents. One of the biggest sellers of magazines in the UK is W. H. Smith. To be successful, a publisher must persuade newsagents and other shops to stock their magazine.

Producing a magazine

Magazines, like newspapers, are all different. However, like newspapers, their individual production processes are essentially the same. A typical production process includes the following stages:

- **Planning:** The editor and advertising manager discuss how many pages the magazine will have. This is called pagination and is decided on the basis of how many adverts have been sold for a particular edition.
- **Writing:** The content of the magazine is produced. Like newspapers, this comes from two sources, the advertising department and the editorial department. Most magazines carry classified advertisements, and the glossy, full-colour format of the majority of magazines offers a good platform for eye-catching display adverts. Editorial in most magazines is made up of a combination of features, photographic spreads, columns, news items and readers' letters. A lot of feature articles are written by

A flat plan is an essential tool for magazine editors

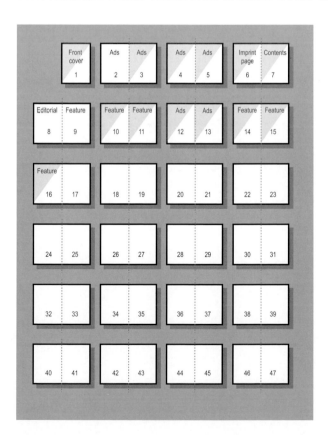

freelance journalists, who are writers who work for themselves and sell articles to several different magazines. Journalists who are employed just to work on a particular magazine are called staff writers. Photographs are often taken by freelance photographers.

- **Designing:** Designers and sub-editors lay out the adverts and editorial on pages. They work according to what is called a flat plan, which is a map of the magazine that shows every page and what will appear on it.

- **Printing:** Most magazines are published in full colour. To produce them, special printing plates have to be made of each page using a technique called 'colour separation'. Pages are printed using only four colours: black, yellow, red (or magenta) and blue (or cyan). Every photograph has to be 'separated' into these four basic colours, using filters that allow only one colour through. This produces four pieces of film, which are laid over one another and exposed onto a printing plate. All the colours needed to produce a full-colour photograph are made by mixing different size dots of these four basic colours. Colour separating and printing are usually done by printing companies, not by the magazines themselves.

Just as newspapers now have an online edition, so do most magazines. The online edition, however, tends to act much more as a teaser for the print edition than it does with a newspaper. One reason for this is that there is far less pressure on a magazine to be contemporary, offering absolutely up-to-date stories to its readers. This means that the print edition will usually maintain advantages over the online offering. One interesting fact that you might like to consider is the way in which magazines that have folded because they are not economically viable have maintained a presence in the market by having an online edition. A good example of this is *Smash Hits* magazine. Popular with teenagers, especially girls, throughout the 1980s and 1990s, the magazine published its last print issue in February 2006. At its height it sold 500,000 copies but more recently circulation had declined to 120,000 before its owner, Emap, decided to close it down.

Comics

Development

You may think comics are something produced to keep young children amused. However, comics are an important part of the modern magazine market and they have a long and eventful history. They are also big business, and not just for children. In fact, in Japan, comic books outsell most leading newspapers.

The first ever issue of The Beano, *published in 1938*

Comics are books of stories that are told in the form of cartoons. They started life as comic strips, which were introduced into newspapers at the end of the

19th century to attract more readers. In the early 20th century, comic strips began to be collected from newspapers and published as magazines in their own right.

Comics really became popular in the UK in 1937, when DC Thompson published *The Dandy*. A year later, *The Beano* was launched and became the UK's bestselling comic.

In America, the 1930s saw the birth of many of the cartoon characters that have become household names throughout the world: Superman, Batman, Spiderman, Wonder Woman, Buck Rogers and Flash Gordon. Most of these characters appeared in comics published by Marvel.

An early Batman comic strip published in the USA by Marvel Comics

Comics have never been aimed only at children. In the 1960s, the adult comic was born. Some of these comics dealt with serious subjects, using cartoons to make political statements. Others were sexually explicit or depicted extreme violence. It was during the 1960s and 1970s that a recognisable comic culture developed, with serious collectors and specialist shops. The introduction of 'manga' comics from Japan into the UK and America in the early 1990s led to an explosion of interest in comics. Manga is a style of Japanese animation.

Cartoon animals were an early development in the history of cinema, and there has always been a close relationship between comics and films.

Many cartoon characters that first appeared on the cinema screen, such as those of Disney, have their own comic books, as do such television characters as Sooty and Scooby Doo. Other comic characters that were created for the page have gone onto the screen, many of them being played by real actors, for example, Judge Dredd and Tank Girl. Japanese comics inspired 'anime' (the Japanese word for animation), which is the video animation of popular manga publications. Even toys, such as Care Bears and Barbie, have their own comics.

The long-running Dan Dare comic strip appeared on the front cover of The Eagle *comic throughout the 1950s and 60s*

Genres

In Chapter 2 (pages 30–32), the concept of genre was examined. Genre is the word used to describe types of media text that can be grouped together because of their shared themes and structures. Genres are very important in the field of comics. Comic genres include science fiction and fantasy, war, superhero and educational. Each genre has its own 'rules' that readers expect to be followed, for example, that the superheroes will always win. Genre influences how the characters are drawn, the storylines that characters are involved in and the language that they use.

Elements of comics

Comics communicate a narrative to the reader through a combination of images and words. The story is told through a series of scenes in the form of boxes. Each box is like a snapshot, in that it depicts one piece of action. In themselves, the scenes mean little, but arranged in a sequence they build up to form a narrative.

The narratives are usually:

- Simple, dealing with straightforward situations
- Action-based, dealing with adventures
- About a set character or group of characters. New superheroes do not usually appear each week
- Self-contained, with a beginning, middle and end. They tend to continue over several issues.

An early Spiderman *adventure published in the USA by Marvel Comics*

The images may be:

- Simple line drawings, as in children's comics
- Artwork that is very complex and even beautiful, as in many comics aimed at adults
- Photographs, as in photo love stories.

The characters depicted can be:

- Fantastic, for example, monsters
- Superhuman, or human with special powers, for example, Spiderman or Judge Dredd
- Anthropomorphic, in other words, animals with human characteristics, such as the ability to speak
- Realistic, either because the characters are drawn realistically, or because the stories are made up from photographs.

The words in comics are usually kept to a bare minimum. They are secondary to the images. However, they still have important functions to perform:

- Words anchor the image – they tell the reader how to interpret the pictures
- Words express information that is difficult to communicate visually, for instance, thoughts and feelings
- Words give extra information, such as introductions that set the scene for the comic narrative.

The Peanuts *cartoon strip by Charles M. Schulz was syndicated to newspapers and magazines all over the world*

Producing a comic

Comic stories are the result of a production process that involves creative input from two types of people:

- **Writers,** who come up with ideas for stories or scripts. They may invent a character and then write storylines involving that character, or they may be asked to write stories involving existing characters.
- **Illustrators,** who draw the cartoon characters. They may come up with the idea for a character, or be asked to draw a character that has been suggested by a writer.

The production process of putting a comic book together is similar to that of a magazine. The comic book is a combination of editorial (in this case the comic strips) and advertising. The editorial and advertising departments work together to produce a flat plan of the comic. The comic strips are designed and placed onto pages along with adverts. The finished pages are then sent to be printed.

Stories featuring physically aggressive female characters are becoming more common in contemporary comics

Comics, sex and violence

Controversy has dogged comics since they were introduced. They have been attacked for corrupting not only children, but also adults. In America in 1954, the Comic Code was passed to limit what was seen as most comics' love of crime and violence. Comic producers were encouraged to create more wholesome characters and storylines. Despite this, comics have been criticised for being:

Violent: Adult comics have been condemned for being too graphic in their depiction of violence. Children's comics have been attacked for treating violence as funny and not showing its tragic effects.

Racist: There have been complaints that some comics, especially those dealing with war, portray people of different races in an offensive way. For example, in some British comics with stories about the Second World War, Japanese and German soldiers are shown in this way.

Sexist: Children's comics have been criticised for reinforcing sexual stereotypes (see pages 44–47). They do this, it is said, by showing girls as passive and well behaved and boys as adventurous and violent. Adult comics have been attacked for sexist depictions of women. Critics say that women in science fiction and horror comics are shown semi-naked and are used only as props for male characters. Some cartoon characters, such as Tank Girl, have gone against this stereotype somewhat by showing a strong female character who is at the centre of the action.

Immoral: Comics have also been condemned for promoting bad behaviour. In children's comics, characters who are well behaved and study hard are shown as swots. In adult comics, violence and crime are often shown as the only way to gain power or enjoy life.

REVIEW

Looking along a newsagent's shelf takes only a few seconds. However, a survey of the print media shows how much work goes into producing just one of the publications that can be seen in the newsagent's. Next time you are in a newsagent's, take down a magazine and look at how much information it contains. Imagine how long it would take you to read every newspaper, magazine and comic in the display. Our society is awash with printed words and the companies that produce them play a major role in our lives.

The birth of KDKA, the first American commercial radio station, in 1919 was a mixed blessing for the early recording industry. Record sales fell initially as people could listen to music on the radio for free. However, record companies soon realised that radio was the perfect advertising vehicle for their products. The invention of the jukebox in the 1930s led to a new demand for records. The 1930s also saw the publication of the first 'hit parade', or chart listing the most popular recordings.

Getting it taped

The next leap forward for the record industry was the development of sound recording using magnetic tape. The German firms BASF and AEG first demonstrated the use of tape recording with their Magnetophone in 1936. The technique was developed in America by 3M, and Ampex produced recorders that could match the quality of recording onto wax.

An early reel-to-reel tape recorder

The 1950s saw the introduction of stereo recording. This involved recording two separate channels of sound onto one tape. It added 'depth' to musical performances on record and led to a demand for improved record players.

Until the 1960s, buying music on tape was not popular, as the tape had to be fed into a recorder by hand. In 1964 Philips launched the first tapes encased in plastic housing, which could simply be slipped into tape machines. Throughout the 1960s, a battle raged between companies that produced eight-track and four-track tapes and those that made cassettes. Cassettes won, and the introduction of Dolby Noise Reduction, which removed the hiss from tapes, increased their popularity. Cassettes were more portable than records, and sales took off, especially when players began to be fitted in cars. The portable tape player, or Walkman, first marketed by Sony in 1979, created an even bigger demand for tapes.

CD and beyond

The search for better sound quality led the music industry to look at the possibilities offered by computer technology. In 1982 the compact disc, or CD, was launched by Sony and Philips. In the manufacturing process, recordings by musicians are changed into digital information that can be read by a computer. The quality of sound reproduction that this allowed was much better than that offered by cassettes at that time.

As the price of CD players fell, they began to dominate the recorded music market. As well as new recordings, companies began to release recordings they had made in the past, known as their back catalogues, on CD. This was seen as a brilliant marketing move, as it led many people to replace recordings they had owned on vinyl with ones on CD: in other words they bought the same recording twice.

A new chapter in the story of tapes began in 1987 when Sony introduced the helical scan recording technique, which had been developed for video, into sound recording. The result was the digital audio tape, or DAT. Before this development, different sounds were recorded onto different tracks that ran parallel to each other on the tape. The helical scan system records sound onto tracks that cross each other diagonally, which provides better reproduction. The sound quality offered by DAT soon led to it being widely used in recording studios, although the price prevented large sales to the general public. Small digital compact cassettes with high-quality sound reproduction were launched in the 1990s.

In 1992 Sony introduced the MiniDisc, a compact disc that can be used to record in the same way as a blank cassette tape. The MiniDisc combined many of the advantages of the CD in a more portable format. However, like DAT, the scale of its success was limited.

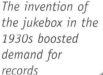

The invention of the jukebox in the 1930s boosted demand for records

In recent years the internet has had an important effect on the way in which we consume music. Initially it was possible to buy CDs at a discount price via the web, undercutting the price that people paid in the music store. Now it is possible to obtain music direct by downloading MP3 files. This downloading of music has developed rapidly for a number of reasons:

- The development of portable digital communication devices such as MP3 players and mobile phones. These are able to store large numbers of music tracks in digital format, which makes carrying a large number of albums a simple and straightforward task.
- The development of broadband internet connections. These allow much faster download speeds than did dial-up connections, making downloading of albums much quicker and more reliable.
- The rapidly increasing availability of free music downloads from the web, both legal in the form of free music from bands and record companies and rather more dubious file-sharing sites that enable tracks to be transferred and downloaded between fans.

Small-format MP3 players such as the Apple iPod and iPod Nano have popularised the concept of 'music on the move'

Music video

Video changed the face of the music industry. Seen initially as a way to advertise records, music videos have become an industry in themselves. Today it is inconceivable for a major, or even new, band to release a recording without a video to accompany it. The complexity of videos has also increased. The first videos usually showed a band performing on stage or in a carefully chosen setting. However, their success led to increased budgets and pop music mini-epics made by film directors.

A major factor in the growth of the pop video was their popularity with television producers. Videos provided TV with ready-made footage that they could simply broadcast for free. They fitted easily into the format of the BBC's *Top of the Pops*, and provided the material for ITV's *Chart Show*, which showed nothing but videos.

It was the birth of the satellite channel MTV, or Music Television, that provided the biggest platform for music videos. Launched in 1981 and broadcast all over the world, much of MTV's output is made up of pop videos, punctuated with

> "Video killed the radio star, video killed the radio star... Pictures came and broke your heart, put the blame on VTR." **The Buggles**

music news bulletins. It is now possible to tune into a range of different MTV channels, each reflecting the way in which the audience for popular music has become segmented by broadcasting different genres of music.

Just as the internet has influenced the distribution of music itself, it has also allowed new bands to showcase themselves direct to their fans through the medium of music videos featured online.

The music industry today

To begin with, recording companies were simply recording companies. Their main product was the reproduction of hardware: they produced records so that people who bought their gramophones would have something to play them on. They had no real interest in music as a money-maker in itself.

Recording companies became aware, however, that they could make only so much money from selling record players. Record players have always been an expensive purchase, and once people have bought one they tend to keep it for a while before replacing it. Realising that the real money lay in the software – the records – the recording companies began to invest money in producing their own recordings by popular musicians. It was this move into the field of music production that led to the music business as we know it today. Big industrial companies now own everything from the factories that make the CD and tape players to the studios where musicians record – and even the musicians themselves. The model for this type of music multinational, RCA Victor, was created in 1929 when RCA (Record of America), together with General Motors, took over Talking Machine Company in a bid to exploit the new phenomenon of car radios.

The music industry has always been dominated by a small number of large companies. This happened because the recording companies bought up independent record labels in the 1930s. (They were known as 'labels' because of the distinctive stickers bearing the company's name that were attached to every record.)

The annual Brit awards are an important showcase for the UK music industry

Today the industry is controlled by five major companies: BMG, EMI, Sony, Universal and Warner. The interests of these companies are global, which means that they are involved in music and other industries across the world. As an example of the sums of money involved in these companies, when it was split from its sister company Thorn in 1996, EMI was believed to be worth around £5.8 billion.

An important aspect of the music industry today is the ability of bands to communicate directly with their fans via the internet. This provides the opportunity for them to market themselves and their music, independent of the huge record companies. Traditionally bands and artists built up their fan base through playing live to audiences. This was often supplemented with the sale of CDs, fanzines and other merchandise, usually on a local basis. This amateur do-it-yourself approach was the hallmark of an important movement in the late 1970s called Punk.

> "The music business is a cruel and shallow trench, a long plastic hallway where thieves and pimps run free, and good men lie like dogs. There is also a negative side."
> **Hunter S. Thompson**

Today, however, bands are able to promote themselves to potential global audiences of many millions online. The availability of free downloads of tracks, streaming videos and fan sites means that fans have much wider access to the band, its music and information about it. The website Myspace has become a popular forum for artists of all types to promote themselves and their music. Both bands that are already signed to record companies and those that are hoping to do so use the site as a way of developing their fan base in order to increase their popularity and the sales of tracks, tickets and merchandise. This direct communication channel between artists and fans means that the artists have much more control over material that is released to the public, and ultimately more control over the image they convey.

The record companies have also been quick to spot the advantages of promoting bands through websites. Many of the slicker and more expensive looking sites are financed by record companies as a way of promoting artists, particularly by word of mouth as fans discuss the sites they particularly like. Another advantage of investing in websites is that record companies can quickly judge the popularity and star potential of an artist through the 'click count' and feedback on their website.

Singers and styles

Singing stars

Just as stars, rather than stories, sell films, so singers, rather than songs, sell music. This is something record companies learnt as they developed: their top priority is to find voices and, more importantly, faces that shift records.

The first and biggest recording star was Bing Crosby. He made his first record in 1926 when the music industry was in its infancy. In 1931 he was signed to CBS Records and became the first nationally famous recorded 'star'. During his career, Crosby recorded 1,600 hit songs, including 'White Christmas', which sold over 30 million copies, making it one of the world's best-selling records of all time.

What is called the youth market for records effectively began with Elvis Presley. Presley became famous in 1956 for singing a new form of music called rock'n'roll. Rock'n'roll was a mixture of blues music and country and western swing. Although the music itself was not created by recording companies, they were not slow to exploit it. Known as 'The King', Presley sold 41 million albums for RCA during his career.

Bing Crosby

Elvis Presley

The biggest-selling album of all time is Michael Jackson's *Thriller*, which has sold 40 million copies. Jackson is signed to Sony. Madonna is one of the biggest-selling female stars in recording history. Her single 'Vogue' is one of the best-selling of all time, and her *Immaculate Collection* album was only the second greatest hits album to achieve a position in the top ten charts. Madonna is signed to Maverick Records, a subsidiary of Warner Brothers. The most successful group ever were The Beatles, who became closely identified with their record label, Apple.

Madonna

Musical styles

The history of popular music has seen the rise and fall of many musical styles. These are types of music that share certain characteristics, such as beat, speed and lyrical style. They have usually been accompanied by fashions in clothing and behaviour. They began with rock'n'roll, which in Britain was the music associated with the Teddy Boys, who wore Edwardian-style drape suits and slicked their hair back with grease. Since then there have been Mods, Hippies, Punks and many others.

The Beatles

Record companies are always on the lookout for new musical styles in order to exploit them. Many people make a distinction between groups that originate a style and those who copy them. They believe the originators are 'authentic' in their musical ideals, while those that copy them are merely commercially driven.

In marketing terms, musical styles are a form of audience segmentation. They can be used to identify types of music consumer. For example, there are general music consumers, who buy records of tunes they like. Then there are specific music buyers, who only purchase a particular type of music by certain types of bands. Record companies judge their performers in terms of their appeal to these different groups.

Classical music – in other words music written from about the 17th century onwards in such forms as symphonies, sonatas and operas – is seen as serious 'art' music compared with popular and rock music, which is often called commercial music. However, classical music has played a big part in recording history and has made record companies a lot of money. Many early recordings

Clockwise from left: Donovan; the Stone Roses; Julian Casablancas of the Strokes; Johnny Rotten, lead singer of the Sex Pistols

were of classical music, and all major record companies have classical divisions. Classical music has become more popular, as indicated by the launch in 1992 of Classic FM, a radio station that plays nothing but classical music.

Getting signed

To be successful financially in the music business, it is essential for a musician or band to sign a recording contract with a major record company. Likewise, record companies are always on the lookout for new performers to sign up.

In order to attract the attention of major record companies, bands and solo artists do any number of the following:

*   **Perform in public** Bands invite representatives of record companies to attend what are often called 'showcase' concerts or 'gigs'. In Britain, bands from the regions will often set up a gig in London to make it easier for record companies to see them.

171

- **Make a demo** This involves making a demonstration recording of their music and sending it to a record company.
- **Release their own record** Many bands pay to release a record on their own label to promote themselves to the public and to record companies.
- **Employ a manager or an agent** He or she promotes the band to record companies. The more experienced the manager or agent is in the music industry, the better. Some managers have become nearly as famous as the artists they represent, such as Colonel Tom Parker, who managed Elvis Presley.
- **Sign a publishing deal** Before the birth of recorded music, music publishers published sheet music. Songwriters and musicians give their work to a publisher who, if they like it, will agree to look after it for a fee. This means promoting the music and making sure the artist receives money whenever it is played. All musicians are supposed to receive a fee every time one of their pieces is sold on record, played live at a concert or broadcast on the radio or television. They also receive money if another artist records one of their songs. These fees are called royalties. Publishing companies are responsible for collecting royalties and subtract their fee from them before passing them to the musician. Signing a publishing deal can help musicians, as it is in the interest of publishing companies for their artists to sign recording deals. Publishing companies actively represent artists to major record companies.
- **Attract attention** Unsigned bands may try anything to achieve a high profile. They will play as many concerts as possible in as many different places as possible, produce publicity material such as posters and fliers, and badger journalists to write about them. The music press plays an important role in 'breaking' new bands by featuring them in their publications, which are read by record company representatives.

Record companies do not simply sit back and wait for musicians to come to them. They go out and look for new performers and try to sign them before anyone else does. Personnel in the company's A&R ('artists and repertoire') department attend concerts and listen to demos in order to spot up-and-coming talent.

"I'm into pop because I want to get rich, get famous and get laid." **Bob Geldof**

If a record company is interested in a band, it may offer them a recording contract. The individual terms of the contract will differ from band to band, but essentially they give the company the right to release all the band's recordings. This may be forever, but it is usually for a set number of recordings, also called 'releases'. So a band may be offered a 'three-album deal', in which they would record three albums for the company and a set number of singles. The contract will also say how much money the band will receive from the sales of their recordings.

On signing a contract, a band usually receives what is called an advance. This is a sum of money given in advance of any record sales which is taken out of the band's royalties once they start to sell records. Advances may range in size from thousands of pounds in the case of unknown bands to millions in the case of established stars changing labels.

For most bands and artists this traditional path remains the most effective way to become successful. However, other means of seeking recognition and success are becoming increasingly popular. One is through an extension of the

TV shows such as The X Factor *offer would-be performers an alternative route to fame and fortune*

The Arctic Monkeys – arguably the first band to achieve success solely by promoting themselves on the web

reality television format in which would-be pop stars compete for the approval of expert judges and the public vote in shows such as *The X Factor*. This type of show encourages hopefuls, both old and young, to achieve fame and fortune by performing on prime television. If the show's judges and the public allow them to progress to the later rounds of the show, they are given maximum exposure to a national television audience and a guaranteed recording contract. Few of the contestants in such shows can claim to have found lasting success and public acclaim (so far), though there have been a few notable exceptions.

Another way of launching a career in the music industry is through the internet (see also pages 00–00). By creating an internet site, bands can market their music direct to their fans without having to impress record companies and journalists. One famous example of this is the band The Arctic Monkeys, whose rise to fame was purportedly due to their marketing themselves and their songs online. Much of their popularity grew by word of mouth between fans who were able to watch videos, download tracks and find out gig dates from the internet. From being a small band known only in their home city of Sheffield, they became internationally known through their use of the marketing power of the web.

Making a recording

Whether making a demo to promote themselves or producing their fortieth album, all musicians need to record their music before it can be sold. This means going into a recording studio, though this may be simply a computer and a keyboard.

A traditional recording studio is made up of two rooms. One, in which the musicians perform, is soundproofed so no other noise can be heard from the outside. The other is the control room, which contains the recording equipment. The recording process is supervised by a sound engineer, a technician who ensures that the best possible recording is made. Sound engineers grow famous for the quality and style of the recordings they supervise; they may become producers, who are much sought after by bands. A producer is someone brought in to oversee a recording and give it a particular 'feel'. The producer's role often merges with that of the sound engineer, as a producer has to know how a studio works in order to get the sound he or she wants.

The recording process usually involves the following steps:

Mic-up Every instrument and singer must have their own microphone so that they can be recorded.

Setting the levels The level at which each microphone records has to be set by the sound engineer.

Laying down the track Recording studios are classified in terms of how many 'tracks' they can record onto one tape; they can be four, eight, twenty-four, thirty-two track or even more. The more tracks a studio has, the more instruments and vocal tracks can be recorded. For a band consisting of drums, bass guitar, lead guitar and vocals, the tracks would normally be recorded in the following order:

- *Drums and bass:* this track forms the base for the rest of the instruments and vocals
- *Guitars:* usually laid down while listening to the drum and bass track
- *Vocals:* usually recorded last. Most recording sessions begin in the morning, when a singer's voice is not at its best. So recording the vocal track is left until later in the day, when the vocal cords have warmed up.

Today a lot of music is produced using electronic instruments and computers. The sounds generated are stored in the computer's memory, which does away with the need for a traditional two-room studio. It also means that one person can carry out all the functions, from playing to mixing. Recording using computers is called digital recording.

The work of a sound engineer

Sound engineers are the invisible people who play a major role in shaping the music that tops the charts. They supervise recordings, making sure that everything runs smoothly.

The sound engineer's job is to manipulate all the equipment in a studio to get the best representation of a band possible. To do this, they have to know the studio inside-out. They have to know how the mixing desk works, the best way to set up a microphone, how to balance sound levels and many other things.

For example, every piece of a drum kit has a separate microphone. The sound engineer has to make sure that every mic is working and recording at the right level. They also have to ensure that the sounds don't 'leak' into one another by using devices called sound gates and compressors.

However, it is not just machinery. A recording studio is a very unnatural environment – it is two enclosed rooms with no natural light and no fresh air. If you have five or six people in a studio for a long time under pressure to produce a good recording, things can get a bit intense. Arguments can break out between members of a band, and it is the engineer's job to keep the peace and make sure the recording gets made. You have to be very diplomatic to be a sound engineer.

Most important, however, is the sound engineer's feel for the music. You may be highly skilled in using equipment, but if you don't care about the music, you will never be able to help a musician record to the best of their ability.

Mixing Once all the instruments and vocal tracks have been recorded they are mixed to produce the version of the track that will be released. This involves combining the sounds using a recording desk. It is at this stage that 'effects' that alter the sound of the instruments, such as echo or distortion, are added. It is during mixing that the producer or sound engineer has a major creative input. They are skilled at getting a certain sound and 'feel' to a recording, and mix every track to ensure it is right. A development of the 1980s was the phenomenon of remixing. This involved the separate tracks of a recording being combined in a different way to produce a different sound. Many producers are famous for this, and bands approach them to do remixes of their recordings.

A technique known as sampling, in which sounds from existing recordings are used to make new ones, was also developed in the 1980s. Combined with computer-generated sounds, sampling removed the need to be able to play a musical instrument.

Formatting Once a final mix has been decided, it is sent off to be turned into CDs, records and downloadable MP3 files that can be sold to consumers.

Making money

The purpose of most recordings is to make money for those people and institutions involved in their production and sale. These include:

- The record company
- The band or performer
- CD manufacturers
- Record shops.

To make money, the price of a CD has to be higher than the cost of producing it. The difference between what a CD costs to produce and what it costs to buy is the profit margin. The profit margin is split between all those involved in the production and marketing process. The biggest percentage goes to the record company. Bands and record companies also make money from broadcasts and performances of their material. In 1999, TV and radio stations paid almost £80 million for these rights.

The charts

The measure of success in the music industry are the charts that show which recordings sell most copies each week. The first music charts were published by *Billboard* magazine in America in the 1890s. They consisted of lists of the most popular sheet music. However, the charts as we recognise them today began when *Billboard* started to publish its Best Sellers in Stores listing, based on information from record shops throughout America. In 1958 the magazine launched its Hot 100 chart, which remains the main chart in the US.

In Britain it was the *New Musical Express*'s Hit Parade, published for the first time in 1952, that pioneered music charts. It listed the ten top-selling records in the country and was compiled by phoning 53 record stores. Today the Official Charts are compiled and overseen by the Official UK Charts Company, a joint venture between the British Phonographic Industry (BPI), the trade body for UK record companies, and ERA (Entertainment Retailers Association). The Official UK Charts Company was established by the music industry to regulate and control the chart compilation process and to ensure that the charts represent an accurate assessment of popularity.

Gnarls Barkley's 'Crazy' became the first song to reach number one before being released on CD

Compiling the charts used to be a relatively straightforward process. When a record or CD was bought, the retailer ran a scanner over the barcode on the product. The information was stored in a file, and every night after the shop closed, the charts' computers automatically telephoned each shop and transferred the barcode files into a central processor. The sales figures were ranked in descending order, and the charts were produced. This procedure was carried out daily and the sales totals grew through the week.

From around 2002, this model has changed due to the emergence of legal downloads which have affected the industry significantly. There is now a chart for downloads (which can be purchased from the websites of traditional high street retailers such as Woolworths, HMV, Virgin, Tesco and many more) as well as iTunes and Napster. Exclusive tracks are often available online before their official release dates and downloads frequently outsell CD singles. In the final week of 2005, over 20 million tracks were downloaded from the internet – aided partly by the fact that online music stores are open 24/7, unaffected by public holidays and store opening times.

In April 2006, Gnarls Barkley's 'Crazy' became the first song to get to number one before it was released in the shops on CD.

Another effect of the download phenomenon is that consumers no longer need to purchase whole albums but can cherry-pick tracks that they particularly like. In time, this may lead to the end of the concept of an 'album' in the traditional sense.

Selling performers

Marketing a performer and their recordings is the major function of record companies. Their aim is to make as much money as possible out of the acts they sign to their labels.

Crucial to the marketing of a performer is their image. This is the way they present themselves to, and the way they are seen by, their audience. It includes the style of their music, the way they dress and what they do and say. Record companies recognise that image is especially important for performers with a mostly young audience. One image that is particularly attractive to young audiences is that of rebellion against society and the older generation. Throughout the history of pop and rock music, bad behaviour by bands has been a way of creating publicity and selling records. From the earliest days of rock'n'roll, wearing leather, taking drugs and smashing up hotel rooms have always been good for business. Although some performers have been marketed in the opposite way – as being safe and wholesome – these performers have always seemed to be more popular with parents than with young people.

Homepage of the Official UK Charts Company, the organisation responsible for compiling the UK music charts

Image is an intrinsic part of a singer's appeal. Top L: Ozzy Osborne; right: Bob Dylan; centre: Dido

Another technique used to market performers has been to set them in competition with rival bands and singers. This leads to fans dedicating themselves to one performer in opposition to another. Image can also harm a performer's success. Many acts are criticised by fans for changing their image, or 'selling out', when they sign to a major record company. The company may insist that performers tone down or emphasise a particular element of their image in order to attract a wider audience. What's more, musical styles and fashion in clothes change quickly, and a band that is associated with a sound or a 'look' that has gone out of fashion can find their record sales falling.

> "Rock stars, is there anything they don't know?" **Homer Simpson**

Performers and their management have also manipulated image to good effect to make successful recordings. Malcolm McClaren generated millions of pounds out of his skilful management of the Sex Pistols, who were at the head of the punk explosion of the 1970s. In the 1980s the KLF Foundation wrote a book on how to make a hit record and proceeded to do so with 'Doctor in the Tardis', which went to number one in the charts. The KLF Foundation later burned much of the money they had earned – £1 million in cash.

Promotion

In order for performers and record companies to be successful they have to make as many people aware of their recordings as possible. They do this using a well-established system of promotional techniques.

Radio

Having your recording broadcast on radio is an excellent way of promoting it. Radio broadcasters and record companies have a close relationship, as they depend on each other. Record companies want people to hear their recordings and radio stations need something to play. A major achievement for a record company is to have its performers 'playlisted' by a big station such as Radio 1. A playlist is a list of records to which a radio station decides to give a lot of airtime by playing them a set number of times during a day's programming. Records that are playlisted tend to be successful simply because large numbers of people hear them. In the 1950s in America there was controversy when it was revealed that some record companies were paying radio stations to playlist their records.

DJs

Disc jockeys, the people who host radio programmes, have a lot of power to promote recordings. If a disc jockey is respected for their knowledge of a particular field of music, such as rock or reggae, their approval and promotion of a record on their show can help sell a lot of copies. The explosion of club culture in Britain has led to the DJs who work in them becoming stars in their own right. They 'perform' at different clubs for big fees and can promote records by playing them as part of their show. Therefore record companies, especially those that produce dance music, are keen to have their recordings backed by club DJs.

Music press

The music press also plays an important part in promoting performers. There are many publications for those interested in music, each serving a particular type of consumer. Newspapers and general consumer magazines also have music sections, and of course record companies supply them with free copies of recordings so they can review them for their readers.

The *New Musical Express* (*NME*), published weekly, keeps readers up to date with what is going on in the music world. It is aimed largely at young people aged between 16 and 30, and concentrates on 'alternative' bands that are seen to be serious about music and non-commercial in their outlook. This does not necessarily prevent them from selling large numbers of records.

- *Smash Hits* was aimed at a younger teenage readership, with features on the latest chart 'sensation' and glossy colour photos. This magazine produced its last print copy in February 2006 and is now published as a website.
- *Q* Magazine is a 'heavy' music magazine for an older audience. It concentrates on famous performers and covers not only the latest releases, but also back catalogues of older recordings.
- *Mojo* specifically targets those interested in artists from the past and in re-releases of their material.
- *Classic FM* caters for those interested in high-quality recordings of classical music.

There are many other specialist music magazines and newspapers. Newspapers and general consumer magazines also have music sections, and record companies supply them with free review copies of new recordings.

Advertising

As with any other consumer product, advertising plays an important role in music promotion. Record companies place adverts in the press, magazines and on TV. Posters are one of the most common methods of advertising. A controversial practice – because it is often illegal – is that of fly-posting. This involves sticking posters advertising record releases on walls, fences and buildings. Sponsorship is another way of bringing in money and advertising at the same time. Record producers often manufacture bands in order to cash in on a musical trend. A particularly successful example is the Spice Girls – a band created in 1994 by carefully auditioning individual members until a marketable product was manufactured. So successful was the product that the Spice Girls sold more than 53 million records and became one of the biggest selling female groups of all time. They released three albums, ten singles and a film, *Spiceworld: The Movie*, which grossed $75 million at the box office.

The music press is a powerful opinion-former

Merchandise

Merchandise is products that carry the name of a performer, for instance t-shirts and jackets. These are a clever marketing device. Firstly, they make money for the record company and the performer. Secondly, they also advertise the performer, as other people see the product and may go on to buy their recordings as a result.

Fan clubs are a useful way of selling merchandise, as are stalls at concerts. Many bands also have mailing lists of addresses built up through pre-paid postcards included in CDs and tapes, to which they send information on new releases.

Concerts

In its early days, sound recording was seen as a way of capturing live performances by musicians – so those who could not attend could hear them. However, the playback quality of music produced in studios soon surpassed that of music recorded 'live'. Performers were then faced with the task of trying to produce studio-quality music on stage. Today, concerts are seen largely as a way to promote recorded music. A band will tour 'on the back of' an album, that is, they make a record and use a tour to sell it. Live albums sell significantly fewer copies than studio-recorded ones.

In the shops

How many people buy their products is of great concern to record companies. Early gramophone records were sold in music shops, along with musical instruments and sheet music. Before long, however, stores began to open that sold only recorded music. Department stores also began to incorporate record sections in their layouts. As well as general record shops, specialist shops sprang up selling recordings of particular types of music, such as jazz or classical.

Record companies, however, needed to ensure that there were enough outlets for their products and decided not to rely solely on independent retailers. They began to buy up existing chains or opened their own. In doing this, the multinational music companies took control of every part of the process, from recording performers to producing the records and selling them. Today, EMI owns the HMV chain of shops, while Virgin has its own successful outlets.

In the 1990s, music megastores were opened. Pioneered by the Virgin group, these shops brought the selling of recorded music full circle. CDs and vinyl records are only a part of the range of products sold in these shops, which also stock DVDs, computer games and consoles, posters, clothing, books and sheet music. This move from record shops to what Virgin calls 'home entertainment stores' has been followed by other music retailers.

REVIEW

The aim of the recording industry is not to make music but to make money. Music is simply the product that the industry sells. To be successful, a record company has to present the consumer with a popular product, such as a band, in an attractive package, such as an album, recorded on an accessible format, such as a CD. The music you play on your CD may have been written by the performer in their bedroom, but, on its route to you, it has gone through a complex industrial and marketing process as part of a multi-million pound business.

JOHN BULL, April 30 1955

'TINGLING-FRESH'
–and you're toughening your gums too

Ice-fresh!
Tingling-fresh! Ice-fresh! SR means sparkling white-ness for your teeth . . . pure sweet breath. And for your gums, that tingling-freshness means even more . . . it's a tingle of health.

For SR does more
Yes, more than freshness. That tingle on your gums tells you that brushing with SR is doing them good. For the tingle comes from SR's Sodium Ricinoleate, a substance that has been proved beneficial to the gums. So brush with SR, and toughen them up to resist infection.
    No wonder SR is the biggest-selling toothpaste of them all!

Ice-fresh, tingling-fresh for teeth and gums

A press advertisement from the 1950s. In 1955 Gibbs SR became the first product to be advertised on British TV

Radio adverts

Adverts are played during most programmes on commercial radio stations. Radio commercials are less expensive to produce than those for television, and the cost of airtime is also significantly lower. This means that more companies can afford to advertise on radio, especially small local ones.

Radio commercials usually take the form of a short presentation using music and speech. Many use a catchy piece of music with simple lyrics, called a jingle, to get listeners to remember the advert. The majority of radio adverts are made by local radio stations that have their own production units. Others, especially those that are broadcast nationally, are made by commercial companies.

Press advertising

A large proportion of newspapers and magazines is taken up by advertising. In fact, some papers are made up of nothing more than adverts. Publishers design their products around what is called 'advertising ratios'. This means how much of a magazine or newspaper will be made up of adverts and how much will be taken up by stories and pictures (editorial). The percentage of adverts in newspapers depends to a large extent on their circulation figures. National daily newspapers tend to have the smallest amount of space devoted to adverts, while small local papers usually have the largest percentage of adverts.

Advertising in newspapers and magazines falls into three types:

Display adverts: these use visual images in the form of photographs or graphics to attract the attention of the reader, and are generally placed by commercial advertisers. They can range from adverts for small local firms, containing a simple company logo in black and white, to full-page, full-colour adverts of internationally famous products.

Classified adverts: these as a rule do not use visual images and consist almost entirely of words. They are generally arranged in columns towards the back of publications and are often known as the 'small ads'. They include things such as births, marriages and deaths, job adverts and adverts placed by members of the public.

Advertorials: these are pieces of writing about companies, describing and promoting their products. They can be accompanied by photographs. By law, such piece of writing must have the words 'advertising feature' printed next to them so that people do not confuse them with news stories.

Top: Chanel advertisement 1996; Middle: Classified ads from Loot *magazine; Right: Example of an 'advertorial' from the 1950s*

Prices for advertising in print publications depend on how much space the adverts take up on a page, and are charged by the column centimetre. Publishers provide potential advertisers with a rate card that tells them how much an ad of a particular size will cost.

Part of an advertising rate card for a London listings magazine. Notice how fees vary depending on the size and position of the advert

STANDARD RATES		SPECIAL POSITION RATES	
Outside back cover	£7,120	**Early Features**	
Inside front cover	£6,760	Half DPS	£6,235
Inside back cover	£5,860	Half page	£3,440
Inside front cover gatefold	£15,000	Third	£2,900
First double page spread	£10,080	Two thirds page	£5,375
Second double page spread	£9,200		
Double page spread	£8,400	**Bookends**	
Full page special position	£5,455	Halves colour	£6,215
Full page	£4,625	Quarters colour	£3,760
Mini page	£3,955	Halves mono	£4,520
Half page special position	£3,430	Quarters mono	£2,910
Half page	£2,905		
Quarter page special position	£1,770	**Broadcast**	
Quarter page	£1,485	Eighth page colour	£1,130
Eighth page	£950	Sixteenth page colour	£565
Sixteenth page	£465	Eighth page mono	£790
		Sixteenth page mono	£395
SPOT COLOUR		**INSERTS**	
Full page	£4,460	Loose inserts (min 40,000)	£44 per 1000
Mini page	£3,615	Bound-in inserts	£55 per 1000
Half page	£2,360	Tip-ons	£60 per 1000
Quarter page	£1,255	Subscription copies	£55 per 1000
Eighth page	£650	Bagged inserts	£ on application
Sixteenth page	£375	Rates subject to VAT at the applicable rate.	
MONO		**DISCOUNTS**	
Full page special position	£4,390	52 Consecutive insertions	20%
Full page	£3,880	26 consecutive insertions	15%
Mini page	£3,275	13 consecutive insertions	10%
Half page special position	£2,275	6 consecutive insertions	5%
Half page	£2,000	**PAID-FOR COMPETITIONS,**	
Quarter page special position	£1,210	**SPONSORSHIP & CREATIVE SOLUTIONS**	
Quarter page	£1,065	Please contact:	
Eighth page	£550	**Derek Pratt: 020 7813 6008**	
Sixteenth page	£315	**Simon Best: 020 7813 6309**	

AD SIZES			
Size	Type Area	Trim	Bleed
	mm	mm	mm
Gatefold	on application		
DPS	249 x 388	273 x 412	283 x 422
Page	249 x 185	273 x 206	283 x 216
Mini Page	186 x 138		
1/2V	249 x 91		
1/2H	123 x 185		
1/4R	123 x 91		
1/4V	249 x 44		
1/4H	60 x 185		
1/8V	123 x 44		
1/8H	60 x 91		
1/16	60 x 44		

EARLY FEATURES AD SIZES	
1/3V	249 x 59
2/3V	249 x 122
1/2H	123 x 185
1/2 DPS	123 x 388

COPY REQUIREMENTS
There are several ways to supply digital advertisements:
1) ISDN (only using ADS in 4-Sight Transmission Director
2) Quickcut.
3) Email (for files up to 3Mb only)
4) Disc.

1) ISDN
Copy for colour and mono advertisements can be sent via ISDN on 020 7637 5717 (providing you have 4-Sight Transmission Director)

Where the advertisement appears in the paper or magazine also affects how much it will cost. An advert close to the front of the publication will cost more than one towards the back.

Sponsorship

Another popular form of advertising that uses the media is sponsorship. This involves an advertiser paying for the right to have their name associated with a media event. This is common with sporting events, when the advertiser's name forms a part of the event's title. Advertisers also sponsor teams to have their names and logos printed on players' shirts, or have hoardings around sports grounds. The idea behind this is that large numbers of viewers will see the names when matches or tournaments are broadcast on television. This is one way firms can actually get advertising on the BBC channels, even though they do not carry paid-for advertisements.

"Advertisements contain the only truths to be relied on in a newspaper."
Thomas Jefferson

The sponsorship of actual programmes on commercial TV stations is increasingly popular. Advertisers pay to have their name shown or read out at the beginning and end of the programmes and on either side of the commercial breaks. So a police drama series may be produced in association with an insurance company, or a high-profile film with a soft-drink manufacturer.

Product placement is a form of advertising that is gaining in popularity. It involves advertisers paying the producers of films to have characters use their products. For example, the main character in a film may wear a certain brand of jeans or drive a certain make of car. The jeans or car will be provided by the company that makes them, and they will pay for them to be used prominently in the film.

These are examples of what is known as covert or hidden advertising, where a product is promoted indirectly to the public.

Product placement: Daniel Craig as James Bond in a press advert for Omega watches

How are adverts produced?

All commercial television, radio and publishing companies have departments dedicated to selling advertising space. Companies that wish to place advertisements contact people working in these departments, known as advertising sales representatives. Representatives also approach businesses and try to persuade them to place advertisements with their publication, radio or TV station.

Filming a TV commercial on location in London's East End

If a business wants to advertise, the next step is to produce the advert. For television commercials, advertisers approach a production company to make the advert for them. This involves a team of scriptwriters coming up with an

idea for a commercial. Once an idea is agreed upon, a storyboard is drawn up. This is a series of drawings showing how the action in the advert will develop. A production team, including camera operators, sound recordists, actors and a director then goes into a studio or out on location and films the advert. The finished product is delivered to the TV company ready to be broadcast in the agreed advertising slots.

In the case of radio, newspapers and magazines, the sales representatives usually contact their own in-house production department. For radio, a script is written for the advert by a copywriter and then recorded in a studio by engineers and presenters. In newspapers and magazines, copywriters work with artists, known as graphic designers, who come up with the images to be used. Once the designs have been approved by the advertiser, they are positioned in the page design of the publication.

Advertising agencies

Instead of looking after their own advertising, many big firms use professional advertising agencies to ensure that they get the best from the opportunities offered by the media. Advertising agencies specialise in handling all aspects of advertising, from designing the commercials to buying the airtime or page space. They are particularly good at conducting advertising campaigns that use all forms of the media.

A typical campaign would involve the following steps:

1   The client contacts an agency to develop a publicity campaign for its product. The client gives the agency an idea of how much it wishes to spend. The contract to carry out advertising for a company is known as an account.
2   The agency carries out research to discover who would be interested in buying the product.
3   Adverts are designed to appeal to the people whom the agency thinks will be attracted to the product.
4   All options for advertising are considered, such as TV, radio and press. A decision is made about which type of advertising is best for the product: this may include just one or all three of the different media.

5   If a television commercial is needed, the agency contacts a production company to make it. Press and magazine adverts and scripts for radio commercials are developed by creative teams at the agency.

6   Agency buyers purchase the best spots for the adverts on TV and radio and in the press at the lowest price possible.

7   Research is carried out following the campaign to see how successful it was in generating sales of the product.

Controversial adverts

Over the years there have been a number of advertising campaigns that have caused controversy. This is often a ploy on the part of advertisers to create publicity for the campaign and bring it more into the public eye.

These provocative ads by Sagatiba and Benetton were deliberately intended to stir up controversy

One company that went out of its way to produce provocative advertising was the clothing manufacturer Benetton. For nearly 20 years, their campaigns were controlled by fashion photographer Oliviero Toscani. In the 1990s he provoked the public, using such images as car bomb explosions, a dying Aids victim, child labour, an electric chair and a black woman breastfeeding a white baby. One of his most controversial campaigns was a series of posters that featured 26 inmates of Death Row awaiting execution in an American prison.

The power of advertising

The relationship of advertising to the content of media products has been the subject of much debate. Critics say that because of the amount of money advertisers pay to the media, they can, if they wish, influence what is shown or printed. They also argue that TV programmes, newspapers and magazines will not broadcast or publish material that is harmful to their advertisers. So, they say, a story about defects in a particular product may not be published by a newspaper if the company that makes the product advertises with it. They also say that the line between news and advertising may become blurred when the subject of the story is linked with a major investor. For example, a new product may become the subject of an editorial feature if there is a promise of a lucrative advertising contract with the magazine.

"You can fool all the people all the time if the advertising is right and the budget is big enough."
Joseph E. Levine

However, the real power advertisers have over the media works in a more subtle fashion. The majority of the media in Britain exist to make a profit. To do this, they must attract as many advertisers as they can and charge them as much as possible. Advertisers are interested in media products because they reach large numbers of potential customers. To charge high advertising rates, a programme or newspaper must prove that it reaches a big audience through viewing figures or sales. This leads to the media producing products not on the basis of their ability to inform or entertain, but to attract large audiences. So if a commercial television station has a choice between showing a documentary about an issue of importance that will attract an audience of hundreds of thousands, or showing a game show that will attract an audience of millions, the game show is likely to be chosen.

A similar process can be seen to operate in the planning and marketing of new media products. The decision to launch a new magazine usually boils down to whether there is an audience ready to buy it. If the publishers can sell a magazine to a lot of new readers, they can convince advertisers it is worth paying to promote their products in its pages. The birth of 'lifestyle' magazines for men grew out of the recognition that men would buy publications dedicated to male interests in the same way that female readers had been buying 'women's' magazines for years. In turn, advertisers used the pages of these new magazines to promote products for men, such as skin care products and high fashion, traditionally aimed at women.

Male lifestyle magazines now carry adverts for a wide range of grooming and skin care products

One challenge that has faced the advertising industry is the fact that many of the traditional methods of reaching a mass audience are on the decline. Traditionally, the popular press or peak time television shows were able to offer advertisers access to vast numbers of consumers. These mass audiences have been on the decline for many years for a number of reasons. People now have a much wider variety of options, not only through the many alternative digital television and radio channels, but also through such alternatives as the internet.

In just minutes, this man will experience the ultimate shave.

To a man, the ultimate shave means a close shave. And a comfortable shave. With Clinique For Men M Shave Aloe Gel, he gets both. Without irritation.

Dermatologists favour aloe to avoid shaving discomfort. Because M Shave is rich in aloe but entirely free of oil, even oily, break-out-prone skins can use it in total comfort.

M Shave pumps out blue. Turns to white lather as it's massaged into skin. The oil-free formula eases the razor's glide. The result – a cleaner rinse-off, cleaner razor, cleaner wash basin. Find it and a fast skin analysis wherever Clinique For Men is sold.

M Shave – a close, comfortable shave. A fresh new feeling.

CLINIQUE
SKIN SUPPLIES FOR MEN

Advertisers have not been slow, however, to see the potential of using some of these new technologies to reach their audience. What has changed is that advertisers are able to target groups of people or individuals with specific interests more precisely. This, in turn, has made advertising potentially much more cost effective. Next time you search the web using a search engine, notice the number of advertising sites that appear or pop up relating to the topic you have searched. This is a highly effective form of advertising because it engages directly with a consumer who has shown a particular interest, which enables an advertiser to offer goods or services that are likely to appeal to this interest.

Similarly, many television channels and magazines are aimed at special interest groups. People who buy or watch them will obviously be interested in a range of products linked to their interest. They are said to be part of a 'niche market'. This means that they have clearly defined and specific interests that advertisers are able to target. In many ways, this is a far more effective method of advertising than paying a large sum for a mass circulation advertisement where only a small percentage of the audience will have any real interest in the product.

> "The consumer isn't a moron. She is your wife."
> **David Ogilvy**

Advertising via the internet and on digital channels also encourages audiences to respond immediately. They can buy by simply clicking a mouse, using the remote control or picking up the telephone instead of having to go out and buy the item in the shops. This encourages what is known as impulse buying, where consumers buy something that they had not planned to and may not really need.

An internet-based advertising campaign for the clothing retailer Diesel

How seriously do we take adverts?

How justified are fears about the supposed grip that advertising has on the media? Advertisers may try to use the media in as many ways as possible to promote their products, but how do audiences use advertising? As we saw in the chapter on audience, many people believe that viewers, listeners and readers are brainwashed by the media (page 70). In fact, the reverse is true: audiences use the media for their own ends and have a healthy scepticism of what it produces. Points that should be taken into account when looking at the power of advertising include:

*   Just because an advert looks good does not necessarily mean that it is effective in selling more products. Viewers may enjoy it purely because it is funny or entertaining and never have any intention to go out and buy the product.
*   People tend to be highly suspicious of claims made in adverts and take most with a pinch of salt.
*   Adverts may be 'invisible'. That is, people may switch channels in commercial breaks or go and make a cup of tea in order to avoid watching advertisements. They may also skip past adverts in newspapers and magazines, concentrating only on stories they are interested in.

The Advertising Standards Authority

The Advertising Standards Authority (ASA) was set up in 1962 as an organisation independent of both the advertising industry and the government, to make sure that all advertisements that appear in the UK are legal, decent, honest and truthful, including those that are broadcast on TV and radio.

"Advertising is speech. It's regulated because it's often effective speech." **Jef I. Richards**

The ASA is funded from the money spent on display advertising (advertising in newspapers, magazines and on posters) and on direct mail advertising (advertising material sent through the post). Advertisers pay a levy of £1 for every £1,000 they spend on display or direct mail advertising. The money is collected by the Advertising Standards Board of Finance, a body that is independent of the ASA.

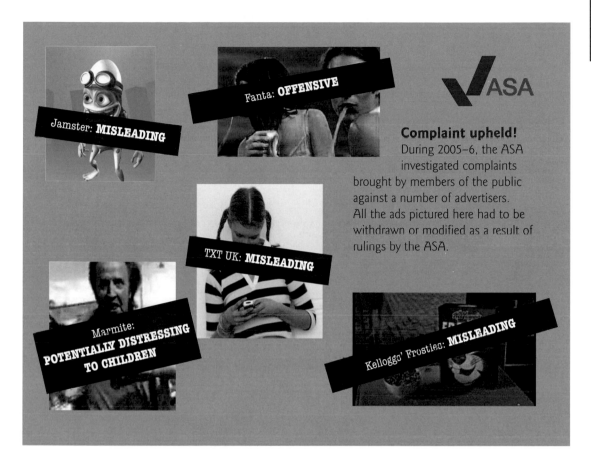

Jamster: MISLEADING

Fanta: OFFENSIVE

✓ASA

Complaint upheld!
During 2005–6, the ASA investigated complaints brought by members of the public against a number of advertisers. All the ads pictured here had to be withdrawn or modified as a result of rulings by the ASA.

TXT UK: MISLEADING

Marmite: POTENTIALLY DISTRESSING TO CHILDREN

Kelloggs' Frosties: MISLEADING

The British Codes of Advertising and Sales Promotion

These codes say what is and what is not acceptable in advertisements. They were drawn up by the advertising industry itself and have two main aims:

- to make advertisers take responsibility for backing up the claims they make for the products in their advertisements
- to avoid causing offence.

The codes are monitored by the Committee of Advertising Practice, which works alongside the ASA, and are in addition to the 120 laws passed by successive governments that apply directly or indirectly to advertising.

The codes include a set of general rules that apply to all published adverts. These rules are based on the following principles:

- All advertisements should be legal, decent, honest and truthful
- All advertisements should be prepared with a sense of responsibility to consumers and to society
- All advertisements should respect the principle of fair competition generally accepted in business
- No advertisement should bring advertising into disrepute
- Advertisements must conform with the advertising codes. Primary responsibility for observing the codes falls on the advertisers. Others involved in preparing and publishing advertisements, such as agencies, publishers and other service suppliers, also have to abide by the codes.
- The codes should be applied in the spirit as well as the letter of the law.

Issues such as decency, truthfulness, safety, the depiction of violence, privacy, guarantees and political bias are all covered in the general rules. The codes also contain a number of rules relating to specific categories of advertisements. These include adverts for alcoholic drinks, cars, medicines and slimming products. They also cover advertising relating to children and adverts making environmental claims. A separate code applies to adverts for cigarettes.

Monitoring advertisements

The government and the European Union consult the ASA whenever they are drawing up policies referring to advertising. Updated statistics on the number of complaints made to and upheld by the ASA can be found on their website, www.asa.org.uk.

If the ASA decides an advertisement is unacceptable because it is misleading or likely to cause offence, the advertisers are told to remove it. Failure to do this can lead to the following:

- bad publicity generated by the report that the ASA sends round of its judgements
- suspension or withdrawal of trading privileges or financial incentives, or the refusal of publishers to sell space to the advertisers
- a court appearance, if the advertisers are referred to the Office of Fair Trading by the ASA for refusing to abide by the codes.

REVIEW

Advertising is the foundation on which most of the media is built, and so deserves close investigation. We have seen in this chapter that media producers get money from two main sources:

- audiences who pay for their products
- businesses who pay to advertise using their products.

The money paid by audiences is usually not enough both to support the production of films, programmes and publications, and to allow them to make a profit as well. Because of this, advertising plays a major role in financing media production. In fact, without funds from advertising, most media products would not get made. This has led to serious concerns about the influence that advertisers have over what the media produces and what we see, hear and read.

11 Radio

Nine out of ten people listen to the radio every day. They listen to it as soon as they wake up in the morning, on their way to work, in the car or on the bus or train. They tune in while they are working, on their way home at night, while they eat their tea or do their homework. Some even fall asleep listening to the radio last thing at night.

Radio is a medium that audiences can consume while they are doing other things. For this reason it is called a secondary medium. Unlike a primary medium, such as television or newspapers, it doesn't demand your whole attention; radio is an ideal medium to use while you are busy with your everyday life. Because of this, it has some interesting functions. For many people, it provides an important source of companionship and acts as a friend who chats to them and keeps them company. It also helps people to concentrate on the tasks they have to do by shutting out the outside world. When you see someone wearing headphones listening to the radio, it is as though they are saying to other people, 'Don't try to talk to me. I can't hear you.'

"When television came roaring in after the war (World War II) they did a little school survey asking children which they preferred and why – television or radio. And there was this 7-year-old boy who said he preferred radio 'because the pictures were better'."
Alistair Cooke

Radio or some kind of background music is often played in shops and factories. It can help make people feel comfortable and soothe them while they work or shop. Radio is like wallpaper, in that it is in the background, making people feel at ease with their surroundings.

Although radio is a popular medium with audiences, especially the younger age groups, surprisingly little attention has been paid to it in Media Studies. Perhaps it seems less glamorous then television, film and the print media, as far fewer books have been written about the medium of radio.

History

Guglielmo Marconi sent the first wireless telegraphic message across the English Channel in 1899. Two years later, he repeated the feat, but this time the message was sent across the Atlantic, from Cornwall to Newfoundland. On Christmas Eve 1906, in the United States of America, Reginald Aubrey Fessenden broadcast the first radio programme, which featured music, poetry and a talk.

However, it was not until 1919 that radio was successfully transmitted in the UK. In that year, a transmitter in Chelmsford, Essex, began broadcasting programmes that contained both speech and music on a daily basis. Three years later, as interest in radio grew, the BBC was born. At first it was organised around the interests of manufacturers and broadcasters, but soon the government stepped in and set up the BBC as a public corporation with its own board of governors and made it accountable to Parliament. Finance was generated through a licence fee. In this way, the concept of public service broadcasting was born.

Radio as a medium

A good way of starting to investigate radio as a medium is to listen to it. Begin by tuning to the FM band on your radio. The frequency is measured in megahertz (a unit that measures wavelengths in cycles per second). Move slowly from the bottom of the waveband (usually 87.5MHz) to the top (108MHz). You may do this by turning a dial and watching a pointer, or you may have a digital tuner, where you press a button and the display changes. As you move from the bottom of the frequency to the top, listen carefully to each station for a short time. Depending on where you live, the number of stations you hear will vary, as will the quality of the sound. If the signal (the electronically coded message sent out from the transmitter) is not strong enough, the reception is often in mono. (Mono sound is amplified through a single channel and is usually heard through just one speaker. Stereo production, on the other hand, splits sound into two channels and amplifies it through two speakers.)

The BBC began broadcasting in 1922

Wave bands

Most radios have both FM (Frequency Modulation) and AM (Amplitude Modulation) wavebands for receiving programmes. In general, people prefer to listen on the FM band whenever possible, because it offers better quality sound and is also capable of stereo and surround-sound reproduction.

Guglielmo Marconi, the father of modern wireless communication

Of course, you need to remember that the brief sample of the stations' output that you have heard may not be typical. It is a good idea to listen again at a different time of day to see if the style and content have changed.

Each radio station aims to establish its own identity so that the audience will recognise it and want to make it the station that they tune to automatically. Different stations have different approaches to broadcasting, in terms of their style of presentation and the content of their programmes. One way in which stations establish their identity is by using jingles. These are short pieces of music which a presenter plays in order to let listeners know they are tuned into a particular station.

"For years everyone looked toward the demise of radio when television came along. Before that, they thought talking movies might eliminate radio as well. But radio just keeps getting stronger."
Casey Kasum

so that information can be added, such as traffic updates for listeners on the move. It is also possible to get access to an Electronic Programme Guide or EPG which allows listeners to search for and find out about forthcoming programmes.

By the end of 2005, it was estimated that half a million DAB receivers had been bought. This means that around one in twelve households had access to DAB at that point. Of course the question is whether one day analogue radio broadcasting will disappear, like its television equivalent. Experts suggest that FM and AM broadcasts are likely to be available at least into the early part of the next decade.

> "I'm glad that even more people can enjoy the show and now even computer geeks from around the world can help feed my ego." **Chris Moyles**

Podcasts

Another important innovation in the way in which radio is listened to is the podcast. A podcast is a radio broadcast which can be downloaded to a computer and transferred to a portable listening device such as an iPod or suitably equipped mobile phone. In order to get access to a podcast it is necessary to have software on your computer such as iTunes, which can search for the podcast you are looking for. Once you have found the podcast you can subscribe, which means that when a new episode of the podcast is created it will be downloaded automatically for you. There are obviously many advantages of this method of listening to the radio. Firstly, it is completely portable, so you can listen anywhere and at any time. Secondly, listeners are no longer at the mercy of radio schedules, and you no longer have to be next to a radio to hear your favourite programme. If you have subscribed, it will be downloaded for you automatically. It also has the potential to open up to listeners the vast archive of material that has been broadcast over the years. Podcasts are also potentially multi-media, so it is possible to have video material podcast, although this is probably better accessed streamed to a computer screen than viewed on the screen of a mobile phone.

The market for portable DAB is growing

Perhaps more important than any of the above is the way in which podcasting has the potential to allow anyone to have their voice heard. Given a microphone and a computer, anyone can access the appropriate online software and start podcasting. As we have seen in Chapter 7, this has important implications for the democratisation of the media and for people's freedom of speech, especially in countries where this has been curbed by repressive regimes. Podcasting is also sometimes referred to as blogcasting, as it combines the features of the written blog with those of the podcast.

The technology of podcasting is in its very early stages, but it has important implications for the way in which radio is produced and consumed in the future. One of the first major uses of the podcast was by the comedian Ricky Gervais, who created and starred in the series *The Office*. He began podcasting his comedy material through Guardian Unlimited, *The Guardian* newspaper's website. He argued that he did not want to use mass media to communicate with his audience, but preferred to create a comedy show where the audience would have to make the effort to come and find him, rather like having to go out to see a film or a gig.

Types of radio station

Radio stations can be placed in broad categories in terms of both their identity and the audience they attract.

Funding

The first division is between commercial radio and what is known as public service broadcasting (PSB).

- **Commercial radio stations** are financed by money from advertisers. They sell advertising time between and during programmes, just like commercial TV stations.
- **Public service broadcasting** refers to radio stations operated by the BBC, including the national stations Radio 1, 2, 3, 4 and Five Live, as well as many local radio stations, such as BBC Radio Cleveland and BBC Nottingham. Just like the BBC television channels, these stations are financed with revenue from the BBC licence fee, although you no longer need a licence for a radio.

Transmission area

Radio stations can also be categorised according to their transmission area, which is the part of the country to which they broadcast.

- **National radio stations** broadcast right across the country, although some regions may listen to them on slightly different frequencies.
- **Regional radio stations** transmit over areas that already have local services. Scot FM, for example, broadcasts to central Scotland, which also has a number of local radio stations.
- **Local radio stations** broadcast to smaller areas. Their transmission areas are often focused on a large city or county. For example, BBC Radio Sheffield and Hallam FM both cover the city of Sheffield and the surrounding area, including such towns as Doncaster and Rotherham. In addition, in some areas there are community radio stations that cover much smaller areas.

Material

Radio stations can also be categorised according to the type of material that they broadcast.

- **Music-based stations:** Many stations are, in essence, music stations. Their main output is music, with some news-related programmes. People listen to these stations chiefly for the music content. Of course, music does not necessarily mean popular or chart music. For example, the main output of Classic FM is classical music.
- **Speech-based stations:** Other stations are speech-based. Their output consists largely of people talking. For example, BBC Radio Five Live provides a news, sport and current affairs service.

Virgin Radio DJ Christian O'Connell

Most stations will have some combination of music and speech. To describe them as music-based or speech-based is to focus on their main output.

New talent
Some local commercial radio stations are accused of only playing music by established bands who are already known to the audience. Critics say that this policy of 'playing safe' means that many talented new bands do not get the chance to reach a wider audience. Radio 1 says that it has a policy of trying to give opportunities to up-and-coming bands. It also uses presenters with a specific interest in one particular type of music such as dance, rap, indie or jungle. In this way, it tries to cater for specialist tastes rather than simply offering middle-of-the-road music that is already familiar to most listeners.

The presenter's desk is the nerve centre of a radio station

The radio studio

Before an audience can receive a transmission from a radio station, someone has to put together the words and music they are going to listen to. This is usually done in a radio studio. Most radio studios are similar in their layout and organisation, regardless of whether the station is speech or music-based.

The nerve centre of any radio studio is the desk, or main control panel, at which the presenter sits. The studio itself is usually a soundproof room. Entry is carefully controlled so that no one inadvertently interrupts a broadcast which is going out live on air. Presenters nowadays rely heavily on the use of computers to help them with their job. Computers have taken over the many technical and fiddly jobs that presenters had to do when studios used large mixing desks to control record decks, CD players, cart machines and microphones. Computer screens can also be used to display up-to-date news and traffic information, as well as receiving emails and texts from listeners.

Programme content

Imagine you have been asked to work as a presenter on a local commercial radio station. What would you have to do to produce a show that would keep your audience listening? The first factor you would need to think about is the time of day your show went out. If your show were a drive-time show, which generally attracts a large audience, you would be broadcasting for people getting ready for, or on their way to, work or school, or who were coming home in the evening. Many would be listening in their cars, so it would be important to include information about road conditions, for example.

During the day, the audience is likely to be made up of people who are at home all day, possibly looking after children or doing housework. Evening radio shows compete with television, so this might be a good time to put out a specialist programme for a minority group.

"Basically, radio hasn't changed over the years. Despite all the technical improvements, it still boils down to a man or a woman and a microphone, playing music, sharing stories, talking about issues – communicating with an audience." **Casey Kasum**

Presenters try to keep a balance between the different elements that make up a show. Talk must be balanced with music. The music itself must be a blend of different types and different moods. Some of it should be familiar to the audience, some of it less familiar. Slow, sad ballads should be balanced with lively, upbeat, happy sounds.

Although presenters can choose much of their own music, they have a playlist of tracks that the stations want to be played most often, which have to be built into the show. Any music used in a show has to be paid for. Such 'needle-time' is paid for by organisations that represent the interests of record companies and performers, such as Phonographic Performance Limited. A presenter, therefore, needs to find other ways of filling up airtime if a show is to stay within its budget.

On a commercial station, advertising slots have already been allocated, so a presenter has to structure the programme around them. Regular items such as news, weather and travel updates are built in, and the presenter may include recorded material from a reporter, who has been out collecting information to be broadcast as part of the show. Called a 'package', it is likely to consist of interview material and actuality (sound-recorded or broadcast, or real events or activities that are actually taking place), with the reporter's voice providing links to guide the listener through the material. The reporter gives the presenter a cue sheet, which is read out to introduce the package.

Having guests in the studio is another possible feature that a presenter might include. Most studios have three microphones (one that is used by the presenter and two extra ones), so that studio guests can contribute to the show in the form of a discussion or interview. This approach is sometimes called a 'zoo format', which means that other voices besides that of the presenter contribute to the programme. The other voices may be identified as studio guests, or they may be anonymous voices of the other people working in the studio, who chip into the discussion or bounce their comments off the presenter. This can produce lively listening, especially if the contributors are able to think up witty, off-the-cuff remarks. For the programme to keep a sense of order and shape, the presenter must be able to control the proceedings.

> "Radio news is bearable. This is due to the fact that while the news is being broadcast, the disk jockey is not allowed to talk."
> **Fran Lebowitz**

Phone-ins have also become increasingly popular. Not only are they cheap to produce, but they also involve the audience in the show and help to keep their interest. Of course, on live radio a phone-in could cause embarrassment if a caller started to swear, for example. Generally, callers are not allowed straight on air, but are screened by a production assistant, who tries to get some idea of what the caller wishes to contribute to the show. In some circumstances, the presenter has a delay button. This means that the transmission of the 'live' show is, in fact, delayed by several seconds, so that any obscene or embarrassing remark can be covered up, with a bleep for example, before the audience can hear it. On-air competitions, where listeners try to answer questions asked by the presenter, are also a useful way of keeping the listeners' interest in a programme, as is the playing of their requests and dedications.

Although a radio show may be seen as quite natural, with studio banter and guests dropping in, a good deal of time and effort go into its preparation. Like many other media products, it takes a lot of work to make the show seem unrehearsed.

Local radio

Today we take local radio for granted. It was not, however, until the mid 1960s that local radio stations were launched. The BBC led the way with Radio Leicester, which started broadcasting on 8 November 1967. BBC local radio stations now cover most of the country.

In many regions, BBC radio is in direct competition with commercial stations, and in areas where there are a lot of people, it is possible to find several stations targeted at a local audience. In London, for example, listeners can choose from such stations as LBC, London Live and Capital.

Whether BBC-funded or commercial, a local radio station is designed to appeal to the interests and tastes of local audiences. Commercial stations tend to play rather more music and carry advertisements for local businesses and organisations. Both BBC and commercial stations carry local news bulletins and provide information and commentaries on local sporting events.

Radio Sheffield is typical of many BBC local radio stations up and down the country. It broadcasts from a newly built studio in the trendy Cultural Industries quarter of Sheffield city centre. Despite its location and its name, Radio Sheffield is at pains to remind listeners that its catchment area includes the surrounding towns of Barnsley, Rotherham, Chesterfield, Doncaster and Worksop – most of South Yorkshire and North Nottinghamshire, in fact. The station has studios in each of these places to ensure that local news and events are covered.

Radio Sheffield organises its daily output to try to meet the demands of its audiences. For example, the Breakfast Show has a focus on news and information and keeps listeners posted with regular updates on travel throughout the area, which includes a busy stretch of the M1 motorway. The morning schedule then consists of two programmes, The Toby Foster Show, broadcast from 8.30 am to 11 am, and then Phone Rony which runs until 2 pm. Toby, a Barnsley comedian, has a show which combines chat, studio guests, audience interaction via phone, text and email and competitions. Toby's style is down to earth and conversational and at times provocative and controversial (at least in local radio terms!). Phone Rony, presented by Rony Robinson, is a phone-in programme. Rony chooses an issue and invites listeners to phone in with their views. Sometimes these are topical and contentious issues. At other times they might be topics that encourage listeners to call in with reminiscences or thoughts on such topics as 'board games'. At 2 pm, Jimmy Carol, 'Sheffield's favourite Scouser' takes over with his show which runs through until 5.30 pm, when there is a half-hour news programme. Jimmy's show consists of features such as Car Karaoke, Jim'll Fix It, the Fab Four at 4 and The Music of Your Life.

Controlling radio

Of course, there are limits to what can be broadcast, for example, material that some people would think was obscene or offensive would not be considered suitable. Also, stations cannot simply broadcast on any frequency that they choose, although there are pirate, or free radio stations, which transmit on empty frequencies.

Ofcom

Ofcom or the Office of Communications took over from the Radio Authority as the regulatory body for radio broadcasting in the UK in 2003. The Radio Authority itself had been set up at the beginning of 1991 to license commercial radio stations and to regulate the material they broadcast, including the advertising they carry. Ofcom is responsible for the regulation of broadcasting generally. Its code of practice, which lays down rules for how broadcasters should behave, covers both television and radio. One important difference between Ofcom and the Radio Authority is that since Ofcom took over the function of regulation, advertising on both television and radio is now the responsibility of the Advertising Standards Authority or ASA. Some commentators have argued that this is a retrograde step for the simple reason that the ASA is a self-regulating body set up by the advertising industry itself. You can read more about the ASA in Chapter 10 (pages 198–200).

You can take a detailed look at Ofcom's broadcasting code on their website. Some of the key areas covered by the code include:

- Protecting the under-eighteens
- Crime
- Religion
- Impartiality and Accuracy
- Fairness.

Each part of the broadcasting code is aimed at ensuring the radio stations do a good job and are fair to the people who listen to them and who feature on their programmes. If a listener hears anything that he or she feels contravenes the code, they can make a complaint to Ofcom. If their complaint is upheld, the station can face a fine. For example, in May 2006 a Kiss 100 radio station listener complained that the lyrics of a song played were offensive and unsuitable for broadcast. Kiss 100 admitted that an unedited version of the song had been played and assured Ofcom that steps had been taken to prevent the same thing occurring in future.

Ofcom also has the responsibility for ensuring that people who set up pirate radio stations are prosecuted for doing so. Pirate stations, it is said, potentially cause interference to existing legal stations, as well as to the frequencies used by emergency services. In 2005, Ofcom targeted 177 stations which were broadcasting illegally, securing 58 convictions. However, stations are often back on the air within hours of being raided.

Planning frequencies

The job of planning frequencies is obviously an important one, with over 170 local commercial stations each transmitting a signal. The airwaves are constantly overcrowded, as stations compete with one another for both space and audience. Part of the office's job is to give out frequencies to stations in a way that avoids interference with other broadcasters' stations. The FM waveband, for example, is divided into sub-bands, of which three are allocated for use by independent stations, both local and national.

Granting licences

When Ofcom grants licences to organisations that wish to broadcast, it must take account of what is in the best interests of the people who live in the transmission area. Choice is the key word here. There are many stations that already broadcast a fairly predictable diet of music and news. A new station might be expected to come up with a proposal that would offer listeners something different in the way of programme content and style.

In addition to all the local commercial stations throughout the country, Ofcom also grants licences to restricted services, which broadcast over a limited area. So far it has granted 2,585 of these for temporary services that can be received by such audiences as a university or college campus, or a hospital.

The FM band
In the UK this extends in frequency from 87.5 MHz to 109 MHz.
FM is divided into sub-bands, used with some exceptions as follows:

87.6–88 MHz	Restricted services
88–94.6 MHz	BBC National and regional radio
94.6–96.1 MHz	BBC local radio (and Radio 4 in places)
96.1–97.6 MHz	Independent local radio
97.6–102 MHz	Independent national radio (Classic FM) and local radio
102–103.5 MHz	Independent local radio
103.5–105 MHz	BBC local radio (and Radio 4 in places)
105–108 MHz	Independent local radio

REVIEW

Radio is often given a low priority by Media Studies students, just because it is easy to take it for granted. Radio is a medium that is often on in the background. People can listen to it without concentrating totally on it. They often listen while they are doing something else, such as homework or cooking dinner.

In this chapter, you have learned that radio is, in fact, a complex medium, which is just as interesting and worthwhile to study as television or film. So next time you find yourself listening to the radio, think about what you have learned about the medium and ask yourself some important questions about what you are listening to:

- What station am I tuned in to?
- What is the station's identity, and how is this established?
- How is it financed?
- What sort of audience does it cater for?
- To what sort of geographical area does it broadcast?
- What rules must it follow in order to carry on broadcasting?
- What do I like about the station?
- How could it be improved?

12 TV News

As human beings, we need to know what is happening in our environment. We need to know, for example, where we can find food and water, where there is shelter, what poses a danger to us, and much more. We need this essential information to survive. However, most of us also have a desire to know things about our surroundings that are not essential. We want to know about other people's triumphs and tragedies, their good and bad deeds, and their loves and hates; about accidents, wars, disasters and famines.

If you were asked to find out what is going on in the world, who is doing what, and what issues people should be concerned about, where would you look? It is a safe bet that you would turn to the news. News is central to our way of life today. It exists to satisfy our desire for vital information, as well as for all kinds of facts, figures, views and gossip.

Television news allows viewers to be 'on the spot' as the story unfolds. Viewing figures shoot up when there is a 'breaking news' story.

LIVE WASHBROOK

MARTLESHAM

BREAKING NEWS   More at sky.com/news
THIRD PROSTITUTE FOUND DEAD NEAR IPSWICH NAMED AS ANNELI ALDERTON

"Television news is like a lightning flash. It makes a loud noise, lights up everything around it, leaves everything else in darkness and then is suddenly gone." **Hodding Carter**

In Media Studies, the term 'news' does not mean simply telling someone about something – news is a product presented to an audience by the media. Most people in our society get their news from television. The main evening news programmes regularly attract large TV audiences, especially when an important or international event has just occurred. Television news is popular because of its ability to let the viewer be there when the action is happening.

People used to be able to get news only through newspapers, which was like receiving a letter about an event. The invention of radio allowed a more direct experience of what was happening, but it was only as good as receiving a telephone call about them. The TV camera allows viewers to look at events as if they were with the camera operator. The sense of immediate reality has been increased by the development of satellite television stations, offering live news from around the world as it happens.

The Sky News team of studio presenters

During the rest of the day, when some of the terrestrials have their morning/lunchtime/early evening news programmes, Sky News has rolling news bulletins: Sunrise (6am–9am), Sky News Today (9am–5pm) and Live at 5 which runs from 5pm to 6pm. At lunchtimes Sky offers a two hour programme, Lunchtime Live, which competes with the lunchtime bulletins on the major terrestrial channels. Sky News also has a programme at 8pm which encourages audience feedback through text, emails and webcam.

One advantage that rolling news offers an audience is the way that it can organise its coverage of major news events or breaking stories. Such stories as a major political row, a disaster or the sudden death of a major public figure will all be fitted into the rolling news format. Sky News likes to think that when a major story breaks, audiences turn to it to find out what is happening. General entertainment channels such as ITV, however, would be forced to reschedule programmes to extend their coverage of a major story, such as a rail crash or the death of a major public figure. The rolling news format also allows live coverage of such events as Prime Minister's Question Time from the House of Commons every Wednesday afternoon, when Parliament is sitting.

The newsroom is the heart of any news-gathering operation, and Sky Centre in West London is no exception. When the studio presenters read the news, the audience is seeing the end of a news-gathering process that has involved a

Behind the scenes, the nerve centre of Sky News is the newsroom at Sky Centre in West London

large number of people and a lot of technology along the way. Every morning, a meeting involving all the senior members of the news team is held to decide what are likely to be the main news stories of the day. Many news stories are known about well in advance, although they are often presented as though they had happened without any planning. Reporters call these 'diary jobs'. They would include a government minister or member of the royal family visiting a disaster scene or opening a hospital. Court cases involving serious crimes such as murder or a celebrity caught drink driving or taking drugs all make good news stories and will be in the news editor's diary. The newsroom will make sure that reporters and camera crews are sent out to cover these events.

Of course, some stories will happen unexpectedly. That is what we tend to think of as news. Major accidents, such as plane or train crashes, floods, riots or serious crimes all come into this category, and there are always members of the team on call in the studio to go out and cover these events.

The morning meeting will discuss the main stories taking place and decide what stories the news bulletins for that day will contain. They also try to decide which is likely to be the most interesting, or 'lead' story, as this will go first in the bulletins. Of course, as unexpected events occur, the contents of the bulletins often have to change.

In a news bulletin, stories have to be organised into what is called a running order. This means that the lead story goes first in the bulletin and then is followed by a less interesting story and so on. It is rather like the front page of a newspaper, where the lead story has the biggest headline and the most prominent position. What makes a story more interesting than another is decided according to what journalists call 'news value'. This is quite a difficult term to define, but you will notice that stories that happen unexpectedly in this country to people who are famous tend to be reported more prominently than, say, an earthquake in a remote part of Asia, even though the latter might have far more serious consequences for the people involved.

Once the morning team has decided what its priorities for the day will be, news crews are sent out to go and follow the stories. A news crew usually consists of a camera operator, a sound recordist and a reporter. The news crew will be looking to make their story as interesting and dramatic as possible, so that the producer of the bulletin will want to use it. This means they will be looking for:

- Interviews with people involved in the story
- Action shots of the event, or at least its aftermath
- A shot of the reporter talking directly to the audience, known as a 'piece to camera'.

In addition, they will need to get some general shots or 'cut-aways'. These are shots that will help to add atmosphere to the report. For example, a report about a factory closure might show workers leaving the premises on their way home. Often the reporter will use these to accompany a voice-over, which is when off-screen commentary is given to explain the story while these images are shown on the screen. The camera crew will always make sure that they have shot more footage than they are likely to need so that they have plenty of material to choose from when they compile the report.

The report is usually put together back at the newsroom using one of the editing suites. It is sometimes necessary to edit a report at the scene, and portable edit suites are available for this purpose. The reporter usually works with an editor in the editing suite to turn the raw footage into a completed news report. The reporter will discuss with the producer how the news report will be put together – the points the report will make, the interviewees, and the pictures to be used.

The reporters will then select the shots and the editor will join them together. Sound, such as a voice-over, can be recorded over any of the sequences of pictures where it is needed. It is likely that the reporter will have been told exactly how long the report should last in order for it to fit into the news bulletin. For example, the report may have to be just two minutes long. If it is any longer it will not fit into the bulletin and the producer may decide to chop the ending or not use it at all.

Sky News' Jeremy Thompson reports live from the scene of an oil depot fire on the outskirts of London

Putting a report together

The reporter edits the raw film footage into a running order. This means deciding on the order of the shots. The reporter selects the shots that they think tell the story best and places them in an order that leads the viewer through the report in a logical way.

Scripts are the commentary that go along with the film footage. This involves writing the words that explain to the viewer what the story is about. The voice of the reporter usually delivers the commentary over general shots, where no one is being interviewed. It is the commentary that holds the report together, as it gives it a storyline with a beginning, a middle and an end.

Once the report is complete, the reporter 'files' it by adding it to the news list. The producer then knows there is a completed news report that can be placed in the running order of the bulletin.

As each news bulletin comes round, the producer has to decide what it will contain. Before the bulletin can be broadcast the news team has to come up with a plan, which involves:

Sky News' Julie Etchingham reports from Suffolk on a police investigation into a series of high-profile murders

- **The running order**, with each item timed precisely so that every minute is filled. While this is going on, they also need to keep an eye out for breaking news stories. If an important news event occurs, it may be necessary to re-arrange the running order to make room for it. It may even mean that a less important item is left out. As well as the news stories that the presenters will read out and the film reports, there may well be a studio guest, such as a politician, to be interviewed. There is also a slot put aside for sports news, which is usually introduced by a journalist who specialises in sports coverage.
- A **script** will also have to be prepared. This needs to include: headlines, stories to be read by the presenters, introductions to film reports and links between items.

The presenters need to have the script in good time so that they can become familiar with it and, if necessary, re-write bits of it so that it sounds better when they read it out. The presenters sometimes have the scripts typed onto pieces of paper, which you can often see them shuffling at the end of a bulletin. Most of the time, however, they are reading the script from an autocue. This is a device that projects the script in large letters just beneath the lens of the camera. A presenter can read the autocue while looking straight into the camera lens so that it appears as though they are simply talking directly to the audience. In the Sky News studio, the cameras are all operated automatically by remote control, so it is possible for just one person, the floor manager, to look after the studio. The floor manager's job is to ensure that the presenters have their scripts ready, to let them know when the cameras go live and to look after any guests coming into the studio.

Sources of stories

Without stories, news programmes would have nothing to broadcast. How do they get their stories? Sources for news stories include:

- **Emergency services:** Reporters keep in touch with police, fire and ambulance services, so that they hear of any major incident as soon as possible.
- **Press releases:** Thousands of organisations send out press releases to draw the media's attention to their news and events.

- **Contacts:** These are people who are good sources of stories. They usually have jobs dealing with the public and so are able to pass on snippets of information.
- **Local councils:** News organisations receive agendas and minutes from local council meetings, which provide a great deal of information that might be of interest to their viewers.
- **Tip-offs:** Members of the public phone in with stories or subjects that they think should be investigated.
- **Other news organisations:** These may be in the form of 'wire services', which are computer systems that transmit updates of news to news organisations for a fee. They are provided by such companies as the Press Association (see the section on news agencies, page 138). The news media use wire services to get stories and information that they may not have the staff or money to cover themselves. Alternatively, news programmes may buy stories from freelance journalists, who work for themselves, or they may simply follow up stories reported in newspapers or other news programmes.

Opening the bulletin

News bulletins at Sky have a lot in common with those of other television channels, but there are also important differences. One big difference is the amount of live news, or breaking news, broadcast by Sky News.

Smartly dressed presenters sit behind a large desk in a studio. At Sky the presenters aim to present the news in a friendly manner. Before the bulletin begins, the audience is made to feel that something important is about to happen. A caption announces the headlines of stories 'coming up' and at the bottom of the screen a clock counts down the seconds to the start of the bulletin. As the bulletin starts, we read that Sky News reaches an audience of 80 million people, in 40 countries, 24 hours a day, and music that reinforces a sense of drama is played. The bulletin begins with the presenter's voice reading the headlines as film is played of the day's events. There are usually three or four headlines before an imposing caption announcing SKY NEWS comes on our screens. The camera then slowly zooms into a mid shot, or talking head, of one of the presenters, who introduces the lead story before a report giving

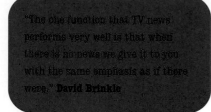

"The one function that TV news performs very well is that when there is no news we give it to you with the same emphasis as if there were." **David Brinkle**

details of the story is played. The presenters usually alternate in introducing stories throughout the bulletin.

Throughout the bulletin the director, producer and their team are working in the gallery overlooking the studio. They are in contact with the presenters through earpieces, a system called talkback which means that if there are any late changes to the running order, perhaps because of a technical problem with a film report, the presenter can be told what item to go to next. Presenters need to be good at reacting quickly to changing situations, for example, if a new story breaks while they are on air or a studio guest has to be substituted at the last minute. In this case they will call up information on 'the wires' (see previous page) which will provide them with the latest news and background on a breaking story. The presenters will also use the internet to find out information. The presenters ad lib too, combining information from the correspondent on the story, from the wires, from the producer speaking through the earpiece and from their own news knowledge.

Using two presenters reduces the risk of boring the viewer and broadens the programme's appeal

Sky News, though distinctive in its own way, is typical of much of the news output from the major terrestrial channels. News presentation is very traditional and the formal nature of the presentation is intended to give news a sense of gravity and importance.

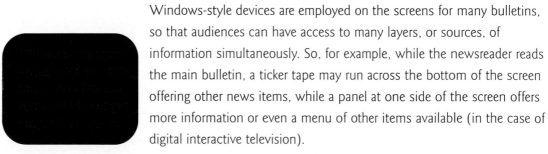

'Breaking' stories allow the news to be broadcast virtually as it happens

When Channel 5 first started to broadcast, it deliberately broke with this tradition. News readers delivered the news perched on the front of desks rather than behind them. This brought a sense of informality to the news. News readers at Channel 5 are closer to the cameras, which means they have a more direct and dynamic relationship with the viewing audience.

There are a number of reasons for the increased informality in news bulletins. It is in many cases a simple device to try to engage audiences with what many see as a boring topic. This is particularly true where television channels are aimed at younger audiences. The Freeview channel BBC 3, created to appeal to a youth audience, features a 60-second news bulletin in which the major events of the day are distilled into a one-minute time slot.

Another innovation in news presentation is the way in which information is delivered. As audiences have grown more used to using computer screens,

Windows-style devices are employed on the screens for many bulletins, so that audiences can have access to many layers, or sources, of information simultaneously. So, for example, while the newsreader reads the main bulletin, a ticker tape may run across the bottom of the screen offering other news items, while a panel at one side of the screen offers more information or even a menu of other items available (in the case of digital interactive television).

In 2006 the BBC launched the Breakfast Takeaway, which allows viewers to download a summary of the news from their Breakfast programme on to an MP4 player. Delivering the news as a video podcast is one of the many innovative ways in which we obtain news.

Many of these changes have been determined by the impact that the internet and other new technologies have had. Both Sky News and the BBC distribute news online, so that people can see it on computers, mobile phones and other devices. As you saw in Chapter 8, newspapers' websites now contain video reports as well as print stories, placing them in direct competition with television news, both in terms of the speed at which news is delivered and the way in which it is presented.

News is an expensive item for television companies to provide. Flying film crews round the world and keeping correspondents on site in key locations requires a large budget. In an age when television channels are always looking at ways of cutting costs, it is little surprise to find that there is now an increased level of audience interaction with the media. Another reason for this is that technology now makes audience interaction much more straightforward. New presenters frequently urge audiences to offer their own views or respond to new items via text, email and phone. Digital services allow a response by pressing the red button on your remote. By engaging the audience to contribute to the programme, the programme makers can fill airtime more cheaply while at the same time arguing that they are encouraging the public to participate in the news itself.

Split-screen presentation is becoming increasingly common on TV news

Similarly, viewers are encouraged to make their own contribution to news bulletins by supplying mobile phone footage of news events they have witnessed. The term 'citizen journalist' or 'accidental journalist' has been coined to describe this phenomenon. This trend started with events such as 9/11, or the London tube bombing of July 2005 when survivors of the bombings recorded footage of the devastation on their mobile phones. These first-hand images of a major news event soon found their way on to screens around the world.

BREAKING NEWS   More at sky.com/news
**POLICE: THIRD MURDERED PROSTITUTE
ANNELI ALDERTON WAS ASPHYXIATED**
Active◯ SKY.COM/NEWS ked as West Ham manager, first team coach Kevi

The mobile phone has also become an important tool by which people can keep up to date with the news. Subscribers to some mobile networks are now able to receive 24-hour rolling news updates direct to their mobile phone. So people are increasingly able to keep up with events taking place, regardless of whether they are near to a television or not.

Regional news

As well as national news bulletins, both ITV and the BBC broadcast regional news programmes. These usually have names that reflect the area that they cover, such as Look North, North East Tonight or London Today. They are usually scheduled next to the national news bulletins or sometimes even form part of it. The format and content of regional news bulletins is very similar to the national news, except that they focus on stories that have occurred in the local area. Many of these stories would not be important enough to be included in the national news, although some of them might be.

Although these programmes contain quite a lot of serious news, the tone of them is often much lighter than the national bulletin. They have a more 'magazine' feel, which might include studio guests, such as a performer who is to appear at a local venue. Like local radio stations, regional news programmes often feature presenters with local accents. It is common to have male and female presenters who seem to enjoy poking fun at each other, rather like some couples do. They might, for example, chat about a particular news story and emphasise the ways in which men and women might react differently to it. They are likely to involve the weather forecaster or sports reporter in their banter. In this way, they establish a relationship with the viewer, talking as though to an old friend, using warm and familiar modes of address.

What is news?

As the study of Sky News shows, the news on TV is the result of a long production process. It is constructed by a group of professional journalists and technical staff, who make the decisions about what the audience will see and how they will see it. Certain factors influence the form that television news takes:

- **Visual impact:** News stories that are visually exciting will often be chosen instead of those that are not. Big stories that do not lend themselves to TV may not be covered, while more frivolous stories that have a strong visual element may be included.

- **Journalistic decisions:** Producers and news editors decide which stories will be covered. Some serious stories may be dropped and replaced with light-hearted ones to add variety to a news programme. Producers and news editors also decide how a story will be told and from whose point of view.

- **Production decisions:** Camera footage that may shed a different light on a story may not be included in a report because it does not 'fit', or is of poor quality. Commentaries may be cut or rewritten to fit in with time constraints.

REVIEW

Television is the most popular of the news media, with millions of people tuning in to find out the latest information. On the surface, TV news seems to be a 'window' through which the viewer sees events happening in the world. However, television news is actually the product of a long manufacturing process, which involves journalists selecting, ordering and editing information and film reports. What the audience sees on the screen is not 'reality', but a representation of events that has been put together by professional newsreaders.

13 Reality TV

Media forms like television need to keep changing if they are to stay alive. If a television channel keeps broadcasting the same sort of material night after night, audiences will soon lose interest and choose another channel that offers more exciting programmes. This need for innovation has led to the phenomenon which has become known as **hybridisation** The word has its origins in botany, where it is used to describe a new plant which has been created by fusing together two existing plants.

Docu-soaps

Docu-soaps are a good example of hybridisation, where two established formats have been fused together to create a new hybrid television genre. As their name implies, they combine the conventions of two different genres:

* Documentaries, which are programmes that present us with factual accounts of issues and events in people's lives
* Soap operas, which are fictional programmes dramatising the issues and events in the lives of people living in a community.

As you can see, both these genres offer us detailed insight into the lives of people. Documentaries, however, are concerned with facts – real events that take place in the world which are recorded by film and television cameras. Soaps, on the other hand, engage their audiences by creating fictional characters and fictional worlds for them to inhabit. Soaps do, of course, rely for much of their effect on being realistic or authentic. This means that they show the world as a real place with real people living and working together in real communities. When an audience watches a soap it is expected to believe, at least temporarily, that the events portrayed on the screen are incidents that are really taking place. Although they are fictional, the world they portray has to be believable and realistic and in consequence easily mistaken for the real world.

"Reality shows are all the rage on TV at the moment, but that's not reality, it's just another aesthetic form of fiction."
Steven Soderbergh

The term 'soap opera' is a dismissive one, as it has negative connotations. It was coined to describe the 15-minute dramas sponsored by the manufacturers of washing powder, which were broadcast on American radio in the 1930s. Producers of soaps prefer them to be called 'serial drama', which has more positive connotations of quality television.

Docu-soaps and the later, broader development of reality television have become hugely popular with audiences, but have also been criticised for saturating television schedules with cheap and mindless material. Any media phenomenon that provokes such a high level of audience interest is clearly of interest to students of the media. In this chapter we will explore how it is that the docu-soap and reality television have not only come to dominate television schedules but also become an important part of popular culture in this country and beyond.

Origin and conventions

It is hard to pinpoint the precise moment that docu-soaps originated as a television phenomenon, but an important programme in the development of the genre was screened as far back as 1974. Directed by Paul Watson, *The Family* was based on an American format. The 12-part series broadcast on BBC featured the lives of a working-class family, the Wilkins, living in a flat in Reading and used cameras in the home for 18 hours a day to record the details of their daily lives.

In the 1990s, another docu-soap called *The Living Soap*, again screened on BBC, followed the fortunes of a group of students living in Manchester who all shared a house. The programme attracted a strong following among television audiences. One of the themes that emerged in this programme was the extent to which people behave naturally when they are being filmed. This is an important issue in programmes of this type. The question is often asked how much the behaviour of people is influenced by the fact that they know they are being filmed by the cameras.

The Wilkins, the subjects of the BBC's ground-breaking fly-on-the-wall documentary series The Family

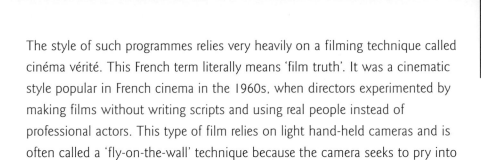

The style of such programmes relies very heavily on a filming technique called cinéma vérité. This French term literally means 'film truth'. It was a cinematic style popular in French cinema in the 1960s, when directors experimented by making films without writing scripts and using real people instead of professional actors. This type of film relies on light hand-held cameras and is often called a 'fly-on-the-wall' technique because the camera seeks to pry into people's lives without them noticing that they are being filmed. It is often said that cinéma vérité is a style of film that portrays life with 'warts and all'.

Cinéma vérité as a style of filming relies heavily on the use of hand-held cameras. When a film maker holds a camera, rather than using a tripod, the effect is to create a lot of jerky movement because the camera wobbles. This effect is accentuated when the camera operator runs with the camera, for example, when chasing someone in an attempt to capture a piece of action. The subjects appearing in the programme are encouraged to ignore the presence of the camera. Directors will often tell them, 'Don't look at the camera' as this is an obvious giveaway to the audience that they know they are being filmed.

"There's a sick sensation in watching humans take risks or fail. We criticise people who stop at the side of a road to watch traffic accidents... in a sense, it's the same thing as that." **Jeff McCall**

The conventions of a docu-soap are that it features the lives of ordinary people, usually in a group or communal situation, such as in a family home or the workplace. In this way it shares the important characteristic of a soap opera of having a focus on community life. It does so over a period of time so that each programme is like an episode of a soap, such as *Coronation Street*. The audience look forward to watching the next episode to find out what has happened to the 'characters' and how the narratives in which they are involved have developed. Usually the characters have some special appeal to the audience, for example, because they may be going through a difficult time, such as problems at work or within the family. Sometimes it is because of a particular personality trait that they possess, for example, people who laugh frequently and see the funny side of things even when they are going terribly wrong in their lives.

Frequent fights between the judges kept audiences firmly glued to BBC's The X Factor

You might like to consider how much of the appeal of docu-soaps is similar to that of soap operas. For example, it is likely that audiences relate to the characters and personalities on many levels. One of the chief attractions, however, is that they can relate to and share some of the emotions that the characters experience in these programmes, especially as the people in the programmes are not wealthy film stars playing a part, but ordinary people just like the rest of us. Just as with the uses and gratifications of a soap opera, audiences can even use some of the situations in the narrative as a means of solving problems in their own lives.

Keeping the audience hooked

Television programmes are often devised to appear as series. This means that they will appear over a period of as many as twelve weeks, usually on the same evening of each week and in the same scheduled time slot. If a programme is to be successful, it is important that it is produced in such a way that it will 'hook' the audience. By doing so it will ensure that viewers tune in week after week and maintain the show's viewing figures. One way that many different types of programmes do this is by leaving the audience with an unresolved enigma. In this way we are hooked into following the programme, simply by our need to find out what happens in the next programme. This serial narrative creates many threads of stories that run through each of the programmes in a series. This running together of different storylines at the same time is called parallel action. It creates for the audience a feeling of importance, because they are able to see what is happening in many different places at once. A major appeal of any docu-soap is this type of narrative, as well as the threads of stories that run through the series, each with its own enigma to be resolved.

The scenarios or situations in successful docu-soaps are usually chosen because of the opportunities they present for conflict. This is one way of maintaining the audience's interest; it also provides opportunities to introduce unresolved enigmas into the narrative. Conflicts themselves are an important narrative convention used as a means of engaging the attention of the audience. Inevitably, whenever conflict arises we, the audience, feel emotionally involved and, in consequence, we are likely to take sides. Many docu-soaps are therefore set in the kinds of situation where people are under stress and likely to engage in conflict. A famous example of this is *Driving School*. This docu-soap featured 55-year-old cleaner Maureen Rees from Cardiff. Her husband, Dave, was trying unsuccessfully to teach his wife, Maureen, to drive. In one episode Maureen managed to run over Dave's foot while driving her Lada, which she called Betsy. The series provided a compelling narrative – firstly because it offered us both conflict with an element of comedy, as the couple constantly argued with each other, but also because we were hooked into watching the entire series to discover the outcome of the narrative – would Maureen ever pass her driving test? (She did on the eighth attempt!)

Another good example of a docu-soap is the long running series *Airport*. First broadcast in January 1999, at its peak the show boasted 8.5 million viewers for each episode. As the title suggests, it is based around air travel and features staff and passengers at Luton and Liverpool airports used by the Easyjet airline. People waiting for and catching flights are often nervous, anxious and inevitably stressed. Low-cost airlines such as Easyjet, featured in the programme, run to tight schedules where things can easily go wrong, putting the airport staff themselves under a lot of pressure. This is therefore a

Ship-board entertainer Jane MacDonald built a career in television after appearing in the docu-soap The Cruise

rich source of conflict between members of the airport staff and passengers, and provides the audience with one of the main attractions of the serial narrative. This narrative is further enhanced by the inevitable airport dramas, including passengers forgetting their passports or key items of their luggage. Their last minute attempts to get these items to the airport before the check-in closes create a narrative tension which engages the audience with the unfolding drama. The show has been sold across the world and an American series based on Southwest Airlines was transmitted in 2004.

Fifteen minutes of fame

You will also notice with the docu-soap format that a number of personalities emerge as the series develops. Individual members of staff emerge as characters that the audience feel they can identify with. This is particularly true in cases where the series reveals information about the personal lives of the participants. The details revealed are often intimate and invariably convey a strong sense of emotion. For example, someone may be about to undergo some life-changing event, such as getting married. A good example of this was on the docu-soap *The Cruise*, set on the cruise ship *Galaxy*. One of the chief characters in this series was Wakefield-based entertainer and singer Jane MacDonald, who was working on the cruise ship. Interest in her as a character increased dramatically when she decided to get married on the cruise. Her wedding to her Danish husband, Henrik, which took place in the Virgin Islands, signalled one of the high points of the series when it was broadcast in July 1998. Such was the interest generated that she was later able to launch a successful television career on the strength of her appearance in *The Cruise*.

Many personalities from docu-soaps and similar shows actually participate in the hope that a television or media career will follow. They go on the show because of the opportunity to be discovered and offered lucrative work in the media. Unfortunately for many, this is rarely the case and more often than not their fame is short-lived.

Other forms of docu-soap

One thing you may have realised is that docu-soaps offer television companies a useful way of filling airtime relatively cheaply with programmes in a format that is known to have an appeal to audiences. The format still remains popular but, as always happens with successful genres, it has developed into other forms. If you look at current television listings, there are a number of programmes that follow reasonably closely the established docu-soap format. One example is *Trauma*, which features the work of London ambulance crews, paramedics and the trauma team at the Accident and Emergency department of the Royal London Hospital. Series involving the emergency services, such as medics and the police, inevitably produce dramatic 'real-life' drama. They also have an appeal to audiences because they mean that cameras are first on the scene at tragic accidents, so we are given a privileged view of incidents which normally take place shielded from the prying eyes of passers-by.

A good example of a long-running docu-soap that relied for its impact on the idea of letting viewers behind the scenes was *Animal Hospital*. Presented by Rolf Harris, *Animal Hospital* ran for ten years on BBC television before it was finally taken off in 2004. The programme showed the daily work of the RSPCA's Harmsworth Animal Hospital. The emotion generated by the plight of sick and injured pets and the hospital staff's help provided a successful narrative formula, giving the programme its long-running appeal.

Reality TV

However, docu-soaps have increasingly shifted into the broader format of the reality TV programme. These allow television producers to continue to use members of the public, often in situations such their own homes. On this occasion, however, these people are advised or helped by 'experts'. The range of problem issues addressed can include home décor, do it yourself, misbehaving children and dress sense. The appeal of such programmes is complex, taking in, for example, an educational function, in which people switch on in order to learn some of the skills featured, through to the sense of superiority to be gained from seeing other people whose lives are such a mess. It is useful to divide so-called reality television into a series of sub-genres, each exhibiting slightly different characteristics while maintaining the central conventions of featuring 'real' people in 'real' situations. These sub-genres include:

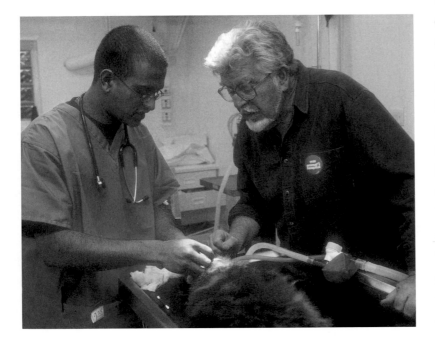

Presented by Rolf Harris, the BBC's Animal Hospital was a favourite with viewers of all ages

Life swap: One popular reality TV format is based on the idea of a lifestyle swap. This requires one set of contestants to change places with others and experience some aspect of their lifestyle which is unfamiliar to them. For example, husbands are asked to exchange wives or families have to go on holidays chosen by other people. In narrative terms, these formats seem guaranteed to provide conflict. Often this conflict is class-based, as people with different values and attitudes are expected to relate to and come to terms with the very different values of other people and groups. So a wife who is obsessively tidy may have to deal with a 'new' husband who lives in squalor, or a family who enjoy holidays that feature cultural activities such as visiting museums and galleries may be asked to play bingo or go to a funfair.

Makeover: The makeover format of reality television itself takes a variety of different forms. The makeover element can either focus on the participants or their homes and gardens. In the case of the former the format can be concerned with the simple transformation of people through changing their clothes, their diet, their lifestyle or their hair and make-up. In extreme cases, people subject themselves to cosmetic surgery in order to 'improve' their appearance. The home and garden makeover format usually features experts in a range of skills such as cleaning, decorating and landscaping moving in and conducting radical improvements to the subject's immediate environment, often without his or her knowledge.

Behaviour modification: The 'stars' of this particular format tend to be children or animals. The basic format requires the parents of toddlers and teenagers with behavioural problems to seek the support of experts to provide help with modifying their behaviour to make it more socially responsible. Similarly, owners with pets that are out of control can seek support from experts in the field of animal behaviour.

Talent search: This format requires contestants to compete with each other for a prize job or opportunity which is on offer. This can take the form of a modelling contract or a record contract, for example. As with other formats, the show relies on the transformation of the individual with the help, often in the form of bullying, of experts called in to show contestants the way to improve themselves in order to win the prize. Another version of this format relies on the use of 'celebrities' who are asked to learn a new skill and compete with other celebrities to win the show. BBC's *Strictly Come Dancing* is a good example of this.

In the BBC's Strictly Come Dancing, *celebrities are teamed with professional dancers to compete before a panel of judges*

Dating: Relationships are a popular theme in television programmes and the reality TV genre is no exception. Utilising both 'celebrities' (often quite minor) and ordinary people, the dating format requires couples to form relationships with one another, often in a controlled environment, so that the audience can see who gets on best. Often a competitive edge is given to this format by creating a scenario in which several people may be competing for the affections of one or more men or women. An example of this format is *Celebrity Love Island.*

Pranks: Television has had an obsession for many years with showing real people or ordinary members of the public. One long-running show both in the USA and in the United Kingdom was *Candid Camera*. First broadcast here as early as 1960, *Candid Camera* was the first of the prank format. It relied on different set-ups to hoax unsuspecting members of the public and film their responses using hidden cameras. A modern-day version of this format is the

Ashton Kutcher programme *Punk'd*, which is broadcast on MTV. This programme features similar types of wind-ups played on celebrities.

As you will have realised, reality television is a broad genre with a variety of different formats. Through all the different types of programme runs a common strand based on the close observation of a group of people in a particular situation. Two of the most popular examples of the genre are *Big Brother* and *I'm a Celebrity, Get Me Out of Here!* In many people's eyes these are 'reality television', largely because their appeal to audiences is so huge. They are programmes that achieve a lot of their appeal through word of mouth as well as through their exposure in the media. This particular format also includes conventions that we associate with the game show. In both cases the series is designed to act as a game between contestants to see which one of them will be the last person remaining after the audience has had a chance to vote off the people they do not like.

The cult of celebrity

Reality TV shows can be further split into two types: those that use ordinary people and those that feature so-called celebrities. Often the two cross over. A good example is the 2006 series of *Celebrity Big Brother* where the celebrities were joined by fake celebrity Chantelle, whose showbiz identity had been created just for the programme. She fooled the other members   of the house by pretending to be a member of the fictional girl band Kandi-floss. Ironically, not only did Paris Hilton lookalike Chantelle emerge from the *Big Brother* house as the winner, but her celebrity status was also established once she left the house and married her *Celebrity Big Brother* co-star Preston.

When is a celebrity not a celebrity? Chantelle, from Channel 4's 2006 Celebrity Big Brother

The artist Andy Warhol famously predicted that "in the future everyone will be world-famous for fifteen minutes". Whilst it is not exactly true that everybody gets their 15 minutes of fame, certainly large numbers of people who would normally remain

"Who needs talent, when the unashamed self-display of the talentless is constantly on offer?" **Salman Rushdie**

unknown to those outside their immediate circle of family and friends have found fame, however briefly, through television shows. We live in a society that seems to feed off the idea of celebrity. Football players, film actors and pop musicians have always achieved fame largely through the skills that they exhibit in doing their jobs. These skills have for years brought the adulation of fans. However, in today's media-saturated world, there is a need to create even more celebrities to fill the pages of magazines and newspapers and supply television and radio magazine shows with gossip. Such celebrities are often created by the media itself, most often through reality television shows. They seem to rise rapidly to fame through their exploits on or off the screen. Just as the media loves to create them, so it also loves to destroy them.

From on-screen romance to showbiz wedding: Peter André and Jordan

An interesting question is: What is celebrity? As we have seen, people no longer need to have a special skill or talent to achieve fame. They are often said to be famous for being famous. Jordan and Peter André are examples of two people who have achieved a great deal of prominence in the media largely through their exposure on the 2004 Series of *I'm a Celebrity, Get Me Out of Here!* Before their appearance in the series, Jordan's claim to fame was as a glamour model with silicone-enhanced breasts and Peter was a singer with a moderately successful career in the late 1990s. Although neither one of the couple actually won the series, their high-profile on-screen love affair created a vast amount of interest among the audience. Their subsequent wedding was another high-profile media event,

with *Hello* magazine paying £1.75 million for the right to publish the wedding photos – double the sum that it gave Catherine Zeta-Jones and Michael Douglas for photographs of their wedding in 2000 and more than the £1m reportedly paid to David and Victoria Beckham.

Another example of a celebrity created by an appearance on reality TV is Jade Goody, who was the third runner-up in *Big Brother* in 2002. Jade became something of a cult figure due to her startling feats of ignorance, believing that Rio de Janeiro was a person and East Anglia a foreign country. She represented for many people the stereotype of Chav culture. After the show Jade's career flourished and she has made many other television appearances, as well as writing a column in a women's magazine and producing her own perfume. Such was her popularity that she was voted 4th in the Channel 4 programme *100 Worst Britons*.

Big Brother

Big Brother takes its name from George Orwell's novel *1984*. Written in 1948, it shows a dystopian or nightmare vision of a future in which people's liberties are taken away by the presence of Big Brother, a surveillance system which relies on two-way television screens to monitor people at all times, ensuring that they conform to the rules established for that society. George Orwell saw Big Brother as a dangerous and negative force which would take away people's freedom and force them to conform. Twenty years on from this nightmare future, we embrace the idea of Big Brother-type surveillance as a source of entertainment. Indeed, the idea of surveillance, rather than being seen as a threat, is seen by many as an opportunity for play.

> "If Big Brother is a one-way mirror on the nation, it is not making us look good."
> Jonathan Freedland, The Guardian

*Big Brother
presenters
Davina McCall
and (facing
page) Dermot
O'Leary*

Getting to take part in *Big Brother* requires a lot of perseverance. Firstly, potential contestants need to be at least 18. They then need to go through a series of auditions to convince the producers that they are the right sort of person for the show. The selection process has to be a rigorous one, as producers want to make sure that the contestants selected will last the course of the show, as well as providing entertainment and interest to keep the viewers watching. Below is some information from Channel 4's *Big Brother* website, which explains how contestants are chosen to take part:

At each location the producers will meet everyone who queues up and select people who stand out to go through to the next stage.

You can do or say anything that will make you stand out from the thousands of other applicants to convince Big Brother why the nation will want to watch you over the summer.

If you are picked to go through to the next stage, you'll enter one of the Diary Rooms and be asked to sell yourself to Big Brother for one full minute.

Advantages for the media industry

The Big Brother format is owned by the Dutch company Endemol. Variations of the show have been broadcast in 36 countries across the world. This ability to develop a format which is going to be popular in several countries ensures that the company that owns the right to the format is likely to make a large profit from doing so.

"Don't put six people in a room and assume it will make good television."
John de Mol, inventor of Big Brother

Series like these create hype through other media publications, particularly the popular press. Newspapers run stories about who is going to be taking part in a series like *Celebrity Big Brother*, as well as stories about celebrities who may have declined an invitation to participate. While the show is being broadcast, newspapers also run stories giving details of the private lives of contestants, often seeking out relatives, friends and former romantic partners to provide gossip. Shows like this, therefore, have the advantage of being self-promoting throughout the media. The interest of the audience is kept alive through the stories in newspapers and magazines, many of which provide the kind of narrative enigma that arouses the curiosity of the public.

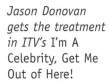

Jason Donovan gets the treatment in ITV's I'm A Celebrity, Get Me Out of Here!

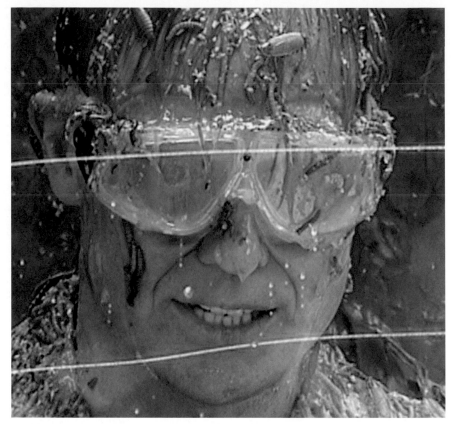

This format brings other clear benefits to television broadcasters. The first and most obvious is the amount of airtime that a single programme can fill. The main target of broadcasters is the prime-time audience on the major terrestrial channels, for example ITV1. A programme like *I'm a Celebrity...* will be transmitted at least once an evening when a mass audience is likely to be attracted. This is one of the advantages of filming the programme in Australia, which is 12 hours behind UK time. The serial nature of the programme creates a loyal following of viewers who will want to switch on each evening to follow the unfolding narrative and see how individual contestants are faring in the show's various trials. *I'm a Celebrity...* is filmed on a vast set in New South Wales in Australia, and a total cast and crew of 450 people are involved in the making of each programme. Both American and German versions of the show are produced using the same set, although ironically the programme itself has not yet been screened in Australia.

Even more advantageous are the opportunities for spin-off programmes that the format allows. *Big Brother's Little Brother* (*BBLB*) is a spin-off programme shown on satellite channel E4. It allows audiences to continue watching after the main show on Channel 4, with presenter Dermot O'Leary providing background and comment on the action. One common feature of the process is to bring in former contestants and other 'experts' to offer their views on what is going on. Additionally the show can be broadcast live 24 hours a day both on television and via the internet for those in the audience who want to see everything that happens unedited. This often means simply watching people lying asleep in their beds. Just as the popular press pick up and promote these programmes, so do both television and radio use aspects of the programmes to fill yet more airtime. Magazine programmes like *GMTV* and *Richard & Judy* will often feature items relating to *Big Brother* or *I'm a Celebrity*... Radio stations will run similar items, often in the form of chat by presenters talking about the programmes.

Another way in which reality TV programmes play a key role for producers is by generating revenue. This is particularly important to the commercial channels like ITV which receive no public funding in the form of television licence fees. Their main form of revenue is through selling advertising space during commercial breaks. One effect of the digitisation of television is that more channels are chasing a limited pot of advertising money. Obviously popular programmes like *Big Brother* will attract big-spending advertisers as long as viewing figures remain high. However, reality TV also provides the opportunity to generate cash through telephone revenues. Most programmes of this type encourage high levels of audience interaction. The obvious example of this is voting by telephone or text to determine some aspect of the programme's narrative. This might be to decide who is asked to leave or stay on the programme or who is asked to undertake a trial of some sort. This audience participation involves using premium rate phone lines, with a significant part of the call cost going directly to the television company. The revenue so generated can be quite significant, and this is often increased by inviting viewers to text or phone in for other reasons, often simply to get a good luck message to one of their favourite contestants on the screen.

Audience appeal

It is clear that the reality television format offers a great deal to television producers in terms of both filling airtime and generating revenue. However, no programme would stay on the air for very long if audiences did not continue to switch on and watch. In 2006, *Big Brother* was in its seventh series and *I'm A Celebrity...* in its sixth. Both had built up and in general held on to a firm audience following. The basic formats of each remained very much the same as the first series, with some innovation to keep them fresh and maintain the interest of the audience.

However, although reality TV remains a popular format with audiences, television companies cannot automatically assume that ratings will always remain high. The third series of *Big Brother* attracted almost 6 million viewers on average, while *Big Brother 7* averaged only 4.7 million.

Chef Gordon Ramsay gets heated in an episode of the TV reality show Hell's Kitchen

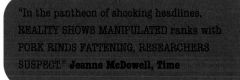

Determining the actual appeal of such formats to audiences is quite a complex business. As we have seen, the serial nature of the narrative is an important factor. Just as people tune into soaps on a regular basis, so do viewers of reality TV. Following the fortunes of individual characters or taking sides in disputes between participants offers pleasure to an audience, which will encourage them to want to tune in on a regular basis. Audiences identify with characters and form allegiances with them. Added to this is the pleasure of being able to vote to keep certain contestants and to get rid of others, which means that, unlike in a soap, individual audience members have the potential to influence the outcome of the programmes. Indeed, there is evidence to suggest that at times audiences collectively vote to keep people who, although not popular or well liked, have personalities which help fuel conflicts. It is these conflicts which are perhaps the most likely source of audience pleasure. Just as audiences form allegiances with different characters, so they also want to take sides when these characters come into conflict with other contestants.

Of course, shows of this type are inevitably on the receiving end of a lot of criticism. Television generally has been accused of 'dumbing down'. This means that the quality of the programmes has deteriorated and that instead of having any kind of educational function, television is designed to appeal to the popular tastes of mass audiences. Reality television programmes are often cited as an example of this dumbing down. Critics argue that they are designed to appeal to the basest instincts of the audiences – their voyeurism, for example. They suggest that the desire to see people humiliated by being forced to undertake trials, including eating grubs and insects, is degrading to both the participants and the audience. It is argued that this is a form of bullying and that reality shows appear to condone this sort of bullying behaviour. The voyeurism extends to sex, with a media obsession with participants' bedtime activities dominating more than one episode of *Big Brother*. In fact, one popular newspaper offered a £50,000 reward to the first couple to take part in televised sex on the show.

One question that is frequently asked about reality television is whether it can be called real at all. Critics of the format argue that the carefully controlled environments and exotic locations in which contestants are placed are far removed from real life. These locations, by their very nature, mean that people in the programme will act differently to the way in which they would under normal circumstances. Within these controlled conditions, producers also create different scenarios which mean that contestants' behaviour can become even more distorted. For example, they may be asked to undertake unpleasant trials – like eating grubs and insects – in order to earn basic privileges such as eals. There may be interventions from producers designed to create tensions and conflicts between people forced together in a closed environment. The very fact that participants are isolated from the outside world also leads critics to call these programmes unreal and the behaviour of contestants atypical of real life.

BBC's award-winning hit comedy The Office was also a sly parody of docu-soap conventions

Parodies

One sure sign of a successful television format is when we see it being parodied. The idea behind parody is not simply to copy an original but to do so in a way that exposes the original to ridicule. Two amusing parodies of the reality television genre are the film *The Truman Show* and the television series *The Office*.

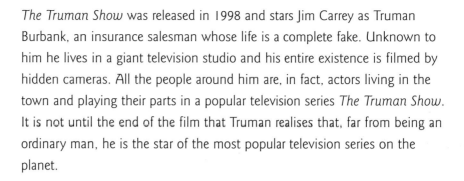

The Truman Show was released in 1998 and stars Jim Carrey as Truman Burbank, an insurance salesman whose life is a complete fake. Unknown to him he lives in a giant television studio and his entire existence is filmed by hidden cameras. All the people around him are, in fact, actors living in the town and playing their parts in a popular television series *The Truman Show*. It is not until the end of the film that Truman realises that, far from being an ordinary man, he is the star of the most popular television series on the planet.

The Office, a BBC comedy series, stars Ricky Gervais as David Brent, Regional Manager of paper merchants Wernham Hogg's Slough office. This comedy assumes the format of a docu-soap which is being made about the office in question. The power of the comedy comes from the character created by Ricky Gervais, who sees the ability of the docu-soap format to create celebrity from ordinary people but fails to grasp how much his fellow workers dislike him.

REVIEW

We looked at the docu-soap and how it developed as a hybrid from two popular genres. We also explored the origins of reality TV as a format. You have thought about some of the different formats used in reality programmes and considered the role of these programmes in creating new celebrities. Finally we looked at the importance of reality TV programmes to producers and their appeal to audiences.